FINDING *the* WAY
Mary-Ann Mey

FINDING *the* WAY

An intriguing **TRUE STORY** of a battle between light and darkness

Mary-Ann Mey

Copyright

Copyright by Mary-Ann Mey – December 2021©

FINDING *the* WAY

The right of Mary-Ann Mey to be identified as the author of the work has been asserted in accordance with the Copyright Act 98 of 1978.

All rights reserved, whether the whole or part of the material is concerned, specifically the rights of translation, reuse of illustrations, recitation, broadcasting, reproduction in other ways, and storage in databanks. No part of this publication may be reproduced or transmitted in electronic, print, web, or other format without the express written permission of the Author.

Published by:
Mary-Ann Mey

Contact:
Mary-Ann Mey
email: marymey123@gmail.com

Edited by:
Diane Thompson
email: di2thomps@gmail.com

DTP:
Clive Thompson
International Professional Book Designer
email: cliveleet1@gmail.com
www.getclive.com

ISBN: 978-0-620-97731-9

Disclaimer

I have tried to recreate events, locales and conversations from my memories of them and in order to maintain their anonymity in some instances I have changed the names of certain individuals, except for the *Personal Testimonies* which are all authentic.

E&OE

Scripture

All Scripture quotations, unless otherwise indicated, are taken from the
New King James Version
(NKJV), Copyright © 1982 by Thomas Nelson.
Used by permission. All rights reserved.

Dedication

This book is dedicated in loving memory of:

Brenda Grace Moffett
9 April 1934 – 1 December 2019

Karyn Cheryl Avis Mey
7 October 1952 – 13 June 2021

Ntombi Prizer Cele
12 August 1966 – 6 September 2021

These special women all played an instrumental part in my journey. They have all since gone to be with our Lord and Saviour Jesus Christ; we hold them in our hearts until we meet again in Heaven.

Brenda

Karyn

Ntombi

Acknowledgements

Clint Mey
Thanks to my darling husband who spent many hours proofreading this book.

Diane Thompson
To my editor Diane Thompson, for your valuable advice and input, final editing and proofreading.

Clive Thompson
To my designer Clive Thompson, for all the advice, guidance and input, for the cover and for walking with me on my publishing journey.

About the Author

Mary Ann Mey was born at the Holy Cross Hospital in Transkei and now lives in Pietermaritzburg, South Africa. She is happily married to her husband Clint for over 24 years and they share two beautiful daughters together, Sharné and Kelsey.

She enjoys travelling and has had the privilege of making memories with her family visiting numerous destinations around the globe. Her passion, vision and life purpose is to inspire and encourage others through the word of God, Her family foundation has always been based on two fundamental principles – "Love and Communication"

Foreword

A life once lived in bondage and in the clutches of a dark world. Late nights and addictions could not fill the gap of loneliness. Trying desperately to be accepted by those around me, I substituted my emptiness with aggression, alcohol and pornography and lived a prideful life destined for destruction.

I met the King of kings – Jesus, on the 19th of April 2008 and experienced the wonder working power of God's amazing love and grace, I was set free. In my walk with Jesus, I have witnessed many testimonies of strongholds and addictions being broken. God has brought wonderful people across my path who have been humbled in so many ways and now live out their faith without any reserve, Mary-Ann Mey is one of them.

I first met Mary-Ann in 2019, when I received a call from her requesting that I accompany her to pray for her friend who was gravely ill in hospital. I was inspired by Mary-Ann's faith along with her zeal for Jesus. Over the past three years I have had the privilege of getting to know Mary-Ann and learning more about her walk with Jesus.

Every journey starts somewhere but not all have a good beginning. I believe that not only will this book highlight the unseen things of this world, but will make every reader aware of the dangers described in Ephesians 6:12 *"For we wrestle not against flesh and blood, but against principalities, against powers, against the rulers of darkness of this world, against spiritual hosts of wickedness in the heavenly places"*

Finding The Way is a true testimony of the transforming power and the unfailing, unmerited love of God and how Mary-Ann and her husband Clint were brought out of the darkness and into the glorious light of Jesus. I trust wholeheartedly that this book will have an impact in the heart and the mind of every reader. I pray that *Finding The Way* will not only encourage you, but show you there is hope, not just any hope, but true hope found in Jesus.

1 Peter 2:9
"But you are a chosen generation, a royal priesthood, a holy nation, His own special people that you may proclaim the praises of Him who called you out of darkness into His marvelous light"

Blessings
Warren Schultz

Contents

Dedication 06
Acknowledgements 07
About the Author 08
Foreword 09

Chapter 1
The Journey Begins 13

Chapter 2
Jet-Setting Abroad 23

Chapter 3
The Search within Deepens 33

Chapter 4
Spiritual Warfare 42

Chapter 5
Reflection Time 142

Chapter 6
Making the Commitment 160

Chapter 7
Walking in the Light 165

Chapter 8
A Humbling Experience 171

Chapter 9
A Trip to the Holy Land **181**

Chapter 10
Testimonies **188**

Chapter 11
Touching Lives **231**

Conclusion 234

Holiday Snaps 237

FINDING *the* WAY
Mary-Ann Mey

Chapter 1

The Journey Begins

'An ordinary family, a supernatural encounter and lives forever changed'

My name is Mary-Ann Mey. As I write I am 47-years-old and have been happily married to my husband, Clint, for over 24 years. We share two beautiful girls – Sharné (22) and Kelsey (20). We are a normal everyday family. Our home has always been based on two fundamental principles – love and communication. As a family, we created a handprinted pledge when our children were still very young, which we put up in our home as a reminder to always give thanks, be kind and considerate to others, to be humble in triumph and defeat, help others as much as possible, respect one another, only speak the truth, listen more closely, sing and dance as much as possible, smile and always make time for family and friends.

Our family has a very close bond and we have truly been blessed as a family to have shared in some of the most amazing holiday and travel experiences all over the world. I have been working in the same department for over 29 years and Clint has worked for his current company for more than 20 years. We are a stable couple and neither of us have had a history of any psychological problems or any mental illness. I just wanted to put this on record before I begin our journey.

In 2018 our lives were turned upside down. We were catapulted to the front row of a rollercoaster ride that we will never forget; an encounter we could never have imagined would happen to us. After reading this, one may say, "Surely this only happens in the movies!" Why we were chosen to experience this, only God knows. We have no regrets.

This is our story...

In 1996, whilst on vacation with friends in Zimbabwe, Clint and I went to see a witchdoctor at Victoria Falls. He arrived in his suit and quickly changed into his traditional outfit. He then summoned us one at a time into his little straw hut. He threw bones on the ground as we huddled together in the small hut. I remember finding it amusing and the more I didn't agree with him, the more aggressively he threw down the bones. Chuckling to myself as I walked out of his hut, I could barely remember what he had even told me because I thought it was just nonsense. He told Clint that he would be getting married over the sea. "What a crazy thing to say!" I thought. We all sat around that evening discussing and sharing our fortune readings with one another. None of us even gave God a thought and we certainly did not realise at that point that only the Lord Jesus Himself knows our futures. It also did not cross our minds that what we had just done was an abomination to the Lord and it also opened a door to witchcraft and the occult, which we had no idea would later manifest in our lives.

Soon after our trip, my dad mentioned that Clint and I should consider getting married on a ship. He thought it would be a fantastic idea and it would be a great holiday getaway. He had told us that he and my mom would pay for the family to join us, should we choose to have our wedding on the ship. We were both super excited about the idea and had not even remembered what the witchdoctor had told us a few months prior. Guess what! On 18th April 1997, we got married on the cruise ship, Symphony, on the bridge overlooking the beautiful Indian Ocean, with our family and friends surrounding us. The seed planted by the witchdoctor was now playing out in our lives. We realise how the devil can manipulate your future by using people around you to advance his kingdom only because you have given him a legal right and a foothold into your life.

Looking back now I can see just how different our wedding actually was. Our vows were made on the bridge and the captain of the cruise liner announced "by the power vested in me by Neptune ruler of the 7 seas I now pronounce you man and wife", my first dance later that evening was with the captain and not even my own husband. I never got to see that wedding footage of those special moments, which my sister Gillian had recorded, of my hair being done by Clint's Aunt, interviews that were recorded whilst getting my makeup done and my dad walking me from the cabin to the bridge, as Clint's mom had accidently recorded over the video.

A few days after our return from our honeymoon his mom called him and was desperate to view it, I asked him to be patient as I hadn't even had an opportunity to watch it, but patience not being one of his strengths and unbeknown to me he decided to take the video cassette to his parents' house to quickly show them the footage and then he planned to return it. He arrived at his folks house just before the start of their favorite daily program "the bold and the beautiful". Whilst he was in the kitchen, his mom decided to start recording her favourite program but was unaware that Clint had already switched the video tapes, and our wedding video was now in the recorder. They all sat down, in preparation to watch the unseen footage when suddenly Clint realized what was happening, he saw a red light flashing on the video machine, he screamed at the top of his lungs and flung himself to the video machine frantically trying to hit the stop record button. Realizing what had now transpired Clint's mom instantly fainted, Clint and his dad rushed to get some cold water and revived his mother and then tried to calm her down, they could not believe what had just occurred. After the initial shock they decided to assess the damage, how bad could it possibly be? They watched Ridge and Brook Forrester conversing right up to the point when the video footage appeared and all that remained was the words "I do", everything up to that point had been recorded over. Needless to say, Clint sheepishly had to come home to give his new wife the bad news, fortunately for him our marriage did not end that day, and today we often laugh about the entire situation

In my early 20s, my colleague lost her fiancé in a terrible car accident. She could not come to terms with it as she was left alone and pregnant. She wanted answers from another realm but, instead of going to the Lord Jesus for answers, she started going to tea and vibe readers. I was quickly sucked into this world and found it intriguing. Soon afterwards I was having my own tea leaves read and was amazed at the information the lady was telling me. Yet again I was opening myself up to the demonic world. The devil knows your past, every thought and spoken word. Thus, he will use this to his advantage and will manipulate situations. The Bible is clear that this dangerous territory is to be avoided.

> **1 Chronicles 10:13**
> *So, Saul died for his unfaithfulness which he had committed against the Lord, because he did not keep the word of the Lord, and also because he consulted a medium for guidance.*

In the year 2000, I went to a vibe reader. Yes, today I realise that is not what God wants us to do. But at the time it felt right.

Looking back, I am not proud of any of those moments, but I was searching for something, totally confused and not knowing the living Word of God. Jesus was reaching out His Hand to me, trying to pull me out of the pit that I was digging myself into. He was calling me, but my spiritual eyes and ears were not yet open. I was blinded by the god of this world (the devil) at that stage. Only Christ can remove the veil when we turn to Him and only then can we see God's glory and see the truth.

> **2 Corinthians 4:4**
> *whose minds the god of this age has blinded, who do not believe, lest the light of the gospel of the glory of Christ, who is the image of God, should shine on them.*

The elderly lady went up and down my arm feeling vibrations and told me that my guardian angel was present. She described my grandfather to precision. She said that I didn't really remember him but that he remembered me as an active little girl, always busy running around. The last time I saw my grandfather, who lived in Beeston, Norfolk, England, was when I was a little girl. He died on the 18th January 1993. She described exactly how he looked and told me his favourite flower was a rose. She described his large hands and told me that I had a piece of jewellery from his side of the family – my engagement ring – which I was not wearing at the time as I had removed all pieces of jewellery before seeing the lady. She told me that my grandfather was telling me to get the claws of the ring checked.

She also mentioned that my grandfather said he would always be with me and that he would be with me at a big function at our house. She told me so many things about past and future events, about my mom, my dad, my brother, Clint and Sharné and asked me if I was pregnant. At the time I didn't even know that I was pregnant with Kelsey.

I believed that God had sent my grandfather to watch over me and that he indeed was my guardian angel – even though I was not a reborn Christian and had mixed thoughts about what I truly believed in. On my way home, I excitedly stopped over at my mom's house to tell her all about the reader's messages and to confirm all the details about my granddad with her. My mother confirmed that my engagement ring was indeed from her dad's side of the family, that his favourite flower was in fact a rose and that my dad had said that my granddad's hands were the biggest he had ever seen. I took the ring out my handbag and asked my mom if she would please be able to get the claws checked at the local jewellery store. At no stage did it even cross my mind that the devil also knows your past or that I was opening myself up to the spirit world.

> **Leviticus 19:31**
> *Give no regard to mediums and familiar spirits; do not seek after them, to be defiled by them: I am the LORD your God.*

I clearly recall my brother's face who at the time was already a born-again Christian. He stood in the doorway of our house as I relayed the message from the vibe reader. He was seriously concerned about me going to a medium and reprimanded me for doing so as he knew the truth. Yet I was so blinded and I honestly thought he was the crazy one. I used to be a scoffer and call him my 'happy clappy' brother. I truly thought he was overreacting and I paid little attention to all his warnings.

A few months past and I received the shock of my life when I got out of bed early one morning only to discover that a diamond had fallen out of my ring. After a few profane words escaping my mouth, I called my mom in tears. I could not believe it. Mom was kind enough to pay for a replacement diamond. I had given her my ring and asked her to take it to the jeweller to have the claws checked. She said she felt guilty for not having done so. I just told her to forget about it and I put the ring back on my finger. The vibe reader's words rang true in my ears and I was left in shock. Again, this shows how very real the spirit world is and its ability to manipulate situations. This was no coincidence; this was the work of the devil but, at that stage, I could not understand how the vibe reader had managed to see into the future. For years I relayed this story to people I met and probably even encouraged others to go to readers, of which I have repented, and today I strongly advise against doing any such thing.

Over the years, I felt my grandfather's presence around me. Years later, whilst showing Sharné a picture of who I thought my guardian angel was, I found the missing diamond in the back of my dressing room table. "What are the chances?" I thought. I was totally blown away by the find, calling my mom in total excitement.

> **Deuteronomy 18:10-13**
> [10]*There shall not be found among you anyone who makes his son or his daughter pass through the fire, or one who practices witchcraft, or a soothsayer, or one who interprets omens, or a sorcerer,* [11]*or one who conjures spells, or a medium, or a spiritist, or one who calls up the dead.* [12]*For all who do these things are an abomination to the LORD, and because of these abominations the LORD your God drives them out from before you.* [13]*You shall be blameless before the LORD your God.*

Close friends of ours whose mother was involved in a spiritualist church invited us to join them one day as they had a medium reader there that day and they didn't get readers all that often in their church.

We didn't think much of it and eagerly joined them, excited to hear what the medium would relay. Kyle was the only one who received a clear message that day and it had to do with the name 'Rufus'. Yet again, we opened ourselves up to the devil's schemes. We have since repented of all these things as I have mentioned before. Thank you, Jesus, for Your forgiveness and the finished work of the Cross.

> **1 John 4:1**
> *Beloved, do not believe every spirit, but test the spirits, whether they are of God; because many false prophets have gone out into the world.*
>
> **Acts 3:19**
> *Repent therefore and be converted, that your sins may be blotted out, so that times of refreshing may come from the presence of the Lord.*

The name Rufus, which is a unique name that I had never really heard of before, would play a role in my spiritual warfare years later, as it was the name of the first road at my mom's house at Amber Retirement Valley in Howick. I recall, during my warfare, even stopping one day, taking a photo of it and sending it to my friend, Kyle.

Going to fortune-tellers, soothsayers and spiritualist churches opened us up to the occult. The powers that come from these practices are from satan and the kingdom of darkness but, like us at the time, most people don't realise this. It all seems so exciting, enticing and enchanting but, to God, it is spiritual adultery which the Bible warns us about.

The Bible speaks about divination which is when knowledge is provided through supernatural means, people predicting your future or telling you about past events and circumstances, a fortune-teller or psychic. The spirit of divination is mentioned in the book of Acts.

Acts 16:16-18
¹⁶Now it happened, as we went to prayer, that a certain slave girl possessed with a spirit of divination met us, who brought her masters much profit by fortune-telling. ¹⁷This girl followed Paul and us, and cried out, saying, "These men are the servants of the Most High God, who proclaim to us the way of salvation." ¹⁸And this she did for many days. But Paul, greatly annoyed, turned and said to the spirit, "I command you in the name of Jesus Christ to come out of her." And he came out that very hour.

They expelled that demon and the lady was no longer able to make money for her master as she was no longer able to tell anyone's fortunes. She was no longer able to channel the supernatural to uncover past and predict future events. God tells us in His Word that we must walk by faith and not by sight.

2 Corinthians 5:7
For we walk by faith, not by sight.

1 Timothy 2:5
For there is one God and one Mediator between God and men, the Man Christ Jesus.

The scripture in *1 Timothy* shows that we should not be seeking information from readers and the like.

Another main avenue of the occult as an entry point is sorcery; the use of magic. *The Oxford Dictionary* definition of the word 'sorcery' reads as follows: 'magic that uses evil spirits'. *The Cambridge Dictionary* definition of the word 'sorcery' reads: 'a type of magic in which spirits, especially evil ones, are used to make things happen'. Sorcery is using different tools to create black magic which can change our physical senses. They may be crystals, charms, magic spells, potions, drugs and the like.

Sorcerers are mentioned in the Bible in numerous books, all with negative connotations, as mentioned in the book of Acts...

Acts 8:9-13
⁹But there was a certain man called Simon, who previously practiced sorcery in the city and astonished the people of Samaria, claiming that he was someone great, ¹⁰to whom they all gave heed, from the least to the greatest, saying, "This man is the great power of God." ¹¹And they heeded him because he had astonished them with his sorceries for a long time. ¹²But when they believed Philip as he preached the things concerning the kingdom of God and the name of Jesus Christ, both men and women were baptized. ¹³Then Simon himself also believed; and when he was baptized he continued with Philip, and was amazed, seeing the miracles and signs which were done.

It is also mentioned in the book of Revelation...

Revelation 9:20-21
²⁰But the rest of mankind, who were not killed by these plagues, did not repent of the works of their hands, that they should not worship demons, and idols of gold, silver, brass, stone, and wood, which can neither see nor hear nor walk. ²¹And they did not repent of their murders or their sorceries or their sexual immorality or their thefts.

There are many Bible verses, both in the Old and New Testaments, that warn against these practices and that they are in fact an abomination to God; but if you are not familiar with the Bible, you wouldn't know this; we certainly didn't.

Our Family Pledge

**Our Wedding on board the Symphony of the Seas
– 18 April 1997**

Chapter 2

Jet-setting around

Fast forward to April 2018. Sharné and I went on vacation to London as Sharné had won a 3-day Contiki Tour to Holland and was departing from London. My mom's hobby and pastime was entering competitions and she had won many prizes over the years. The mantle had now been passed onto Sharné who became an avid competition scouter and she started winning some amazing holiday trips and prizes.

Arriving in London, we decided to visit my Uncle Neville and his partner, Sally. He fetched us from the train station and we made our way to Beeston to visit grandad's and granny's gravesites. Just before we arrived there, Sharné received a call. It turned out that she had won a competition – a trip to Bali. We both screamed with excitement and poor uncle Neville had no idea what was going on. I felt it was sign from my guardian angel, my grandfather, whose grave I was about to visit. My mom had said it was her favourite place in all her travels and the fact that I was so close to my grandfather's grave made me think that it was a definite sign. We took some pictures of Beeston village and then headed to the graveyard. This was a very special moment for me. My grandfather and grandmother were laid to rest in a beautiful English countryside church ground. I felt at peace there.

The following evening Uncle Neville and Sally took us out for dinner to a lovely country pub called *The Bell*. It was just up the road, so we walked there. I shared my story with them over dinner. Truthfully, I was a bit nervous and apprehensive to tell them all about the fortune-tellers / vibe readers whom I had been to as some people react very negatively to this and rightfully so – but at the time I didn't understand that.

My Uncle's reaction took me by surprise. He said I could not have asked for a kinder and better guardian angel. He didn't look at me as if I was crazy; he was not angry or disappointed in me for going to the vibe reader. My granddad was a very kind, loving man and a devout Christian. We all cried at the table that night as I relayed my story and memories of grandad came flooding to Uncle Neville. It was the first time in my life I had gone out for a nice meal that landed up bringing everyone to tears.

Whilst having dinner, Sally asked me if I believed in feathers. I told her I didn't know anything about feathers besides a story I had seen on TV about Reeva Steenkamp's mother saying she felt that her daughter Reeva was sending her white feathers as she saw them everywhere. The feathers she said were a sign from her daughter, telling her she was okay and safe in heaven. Sally then continued to tell me she had found it strange that in the morning she had seen a white feather on her computer keyboard. I didn't really know what she meant at the time but when we got back to their home, I googled the meaning of a white feather and it read: "White feather – sign of faith and protection. It is a sign from your angel that they are well and safe in heaven". I felt warm and at peace and immediately thought that my grandfather was with me and was safe in heaven, just as the vibe reader from years earlier had said.

There are many scriptures in the Bible that teach us about

angels and how God used angels to converse with people in the Bible. God used the angels to provide protection, to provide direction, to provide encouragement and to instruct His people as to what to do. Therefore, He will still be using His angels today to work in our lives. However, we are not to worship angels, pray to angels or idolise them or to be confused in any way about who the angels really are.

> **Revelation 22:8-9**
> *⁸Now I, John, saw and heard these things. And when I heard and saw, I fell down to worship before the feet of the angel who showed me these things. ⁹Then he said to me, "See that you do not do that. For I am your fellow servant, and of your brethren the prophets, and of those who keep the words of this book. Worship God."*

Our trip to London flashed by and before we knew it, Sharné and I were on a plane to Bali. To our surprise, we had been bumped up to business class!! Wow wow wow! I had to pinch myself the entire flight. Sipping on champagne with legs outstretched, I thought about how lucky we were. Even though this was a perfect opportunity to catch a few winks, the excitement of it all kept sleep at bay. There is a first time for everything and I wasn't about to let this once-in-a-lifetime opportunity go by without making the most of every second. I couldn't get the smile off my face.

Landing at my mom's favourite destination intrigued me. All her travel stories of the wonderful people and the rich Balinese culture began to replay in my mind. I wanted to experience for myself just what all the fuss was about. After just a few days there, I could see why she loved Bali so much. The people were very kind and humble; a relatively poor country with a hard-work ethic.

Honestly, we were caught up with all the rituals and ceremonies they perform, giving daily offerings to their gods – flowers, money, certain foods and asking for favour and blessings. The Balinese culture is easy to get swept up in. They have a Hindu-Buddhist religion. We were taken to a dance ceremony called a *kecak* dance (fire dance) a trance – an inducing exorcism dance relaying a Hindu story. It was very over the top for us and we really didn't understand what was going on but, looking back now, it clearly was a place where one would open oneself to the demonic spirit realm.

At the time, we found their beliefs and customs very interesting. I was in a place in my own life where I was very confused about my own beliefs and jumped on anything that tickled my fancy. Flip-flopping from one belief to another, on the one hand, I wanted to go to church and was trying to convince Clint and the girls to go with me. On the other hand, I was desperate to go to the Buddhist retreat in Ixopo with my sister. I was very confused as to what exactly I believed in but I continued to search for the truth.

We were also taken to a beautiful rock formation in the sea called *Tanah Lot Temple,* the work of a 16th century high priest who spread the teaching of Hinduism, making it a holy place of worship for their sea gods.

Sharné and I followed the rituals and offered money to the sea gods and washed our heads with the water that flowed from the rocks. Immediately thereafter, Sharné said she was not happy about doing that; she knew it was wrong and clearly not of God. Something deep inside her was pricking her conscience. So, even though she was not yet a believer, she knew the truth, which clearly demonstrates that God gives us all something in our spirit man that knows right from wrong. He gives us wisdom but also freewill. That practice disturbed her until she repented of it and prayed for forgiveness months later. I, too, months later repented of this practice and many more and I thank God for His mercy, grace and forgiveness.

Isaiah 45:5
I am the Lord, and there is no other; There is no God besides Me...

God is very clear in His Word about His thoughts towards making offerings of any kind to any false gods. We are blessed to have such a forgiving and merciful Father in Heaven whose arms are always open, ready to receive us.

Exodus 20:3
You shall have no other gods before Me.

1 Corinthians 10:20
Rather, that the things which the Gentiles sacrifice they sacrifice to demons and not to God, and I do not want you to have fellowship with demons.

Clint and Kelsey had managed to secure cheap flights to Bali and they wanted to surprise us – very special – as we were able to celebrate our 21st wedding anniversary together in an extremely romantic setting. I dragged Clint around all the curio shops in an attempt to buy gifts for family and friends back home. My sister, Gillian, had asked me to buy her a wooden buddha idol. I was on the lookout for one for her. When I found the perfect little idol for my sister, I wanted one for myself. Clint was not that enthusiastic about buying one for our home but didn't really make too much fuss about it. I think he just wanted to keep the peace, if the truth be told, but that idol made him feel uncomfortable from the moment I purchased it. By purchasing these idols, we are investing in an ancient spiritual realm that is part of the idolatrous kingdom of darkness.

Psalm 97:7
Let all be put to shame who serve carved images, Who boast of idols. Worship Him, all you gods.

Isaiah 2:8
Their land is also full of idols; They worship the work of their own hands, That which their own fingers have made.

The buddha idol was placed on our mantle for all to see when you walked into our home. It was supposed to represent protection. Today I question who exactly it was protecting us from. We need to be very careful of items we bring into our homes and the attachment that they have to the spirit realm. Over the past two years, I have listened to great men and women of God talking on this exact subject such as Derek Prince and an ex-new age teacher, Doreen Virtue. They warn us to be very careful what you buy and bring into your home and gardens. Objects such as sun gods, evil eyes, dream catchers, new age books, books on magic, angel cards and angel board games can open a doorway to the spiritual realm and to demonic attacks and they are in direct opposition to God's Word. Destroy them and repent. Don't give the enemy any rights to your life and anoint your home with oil in the Name of the Father, The Son and the Holy Spirit.

Deuteronomy 7:26
Do not bring any detestable objects into your home, for then you will be destroyed, just like them. You must utterly detest such things, for they are set apart for destruction.

I left Bali with a nagging feeling to release my dad's ashes as one of our tour guides had planted the seed in my mind. However, the opportunity for all us siblings being together at once to scatter his ashes had not yet materialised.

In June 2018, I accompanied Sharné to the David Livingstone Hotel in Zambia – another holiday she had won. The Lord was blessing us abundantly and teaching me valuable life lessons along the way. I had no idea who David Livingstone was and what an amazing man of God he was. He was born in Blantyre in Scotland into a Christian family and, after training as a medical doctor in Glasgow, he joined the London Missionary Society. It was through that organisation that he met the South African based missionary, Robert Moffat, who encouraged David to join him in South Africa. He arrived in Cape Town in 1840 and joined Moffat's mission at Kuruman and landed up marrying Moffat's daughter, Mary. David explored Africa spreading the good news of Jesus and sharing his strong Christian faith. My maiden name is Moffett – just spelt differently – but this intrigued me about this story.

David Livingstone reached the Victoria Falls in 1855 and was the first person to bring them to the attention of the western world, we were able to see the monument at the falls that was dedicated to him for his achievements and for his anti-slavery work for which he also received many awards and accolades. He was a man with a mission, following the great commission which we are taught in the scriptures.

> **Mark 16:15**
> *He said to them, "Go into all the world and preach the gospel to every creature.*

We have a lot to learn in this modern mixed up world from mighty men like David Livingstone. Sharné and I loved exploring the falls and experiencing the mighty power of the raging water and witnessing the beauty of the rainbows that were formed against the rock faces, we also had the privilege of going on a microlight flight over the falls, giving us a bird's eye view of one of Gods magnificent masterpieces. We reclined on the Lady Livingstone cruise whilst sipping sundowners watching the magnificent sunset on the Zambezi River.

During the next few months I started reading the *Vigilant Citizen* on line, a good friend of mine had mentioned it to me as we had often discussed all the evil in this world and we both agreed the world was in a very dark place and getting worse by the day, believing that the devil was working overtime creating all the chaos, we discussed all kinds of topics – how satan was blinding people and desensitizing us preparing us for his onslaught, the world was wicked and I couldn't believe how the media and famous stars had bought into his lies.

Strange, because I wasn't even a Christian at this stage, but I knew if satan was real and I could see his work in play I came to the realization that there must then be a mightier and a more powerful God. I always knew there was something out there I just didn't know what. My colleagues often remind me that even though I wasn't a Christian I would constantly tell them to not get involved in any bribery or corruption as the "man upstairs was watching", and that they would have to answer one day, they told me that during the more than 20 years that I had worked with them they said that they thank me for those constant reminders as they were tempted many times but never once took the bait.

Sharne Mey is 😁 feeling fantastic.
06 Apr 2018 · 🌐

So we are off to an amazing Bali adventure next week ✈️🌍😍💚 **Mary-Ann Moffett Mey** can't wait 🍸💄

 Datsun South Africa is 😁 feeling excited with **Sharne Mey** and **Shirin Vawda**.
06 Apr 2018 · 🌐

Signed, sealed and yet to be delivered! The official winners of #DatsunLove are Sharne Mey (1st prize), Shirin Vawda (2nd prize)... See more

Competition Winners!

Sipping champagne while travelling business class

Bali, Indonesia – April 2018

Zambia June 2018, flying over Victoria Falls

Chapter 3

The Search within deepens

In August 2018, I was researching in depth about the secret society called The Illuminati and a famous singer's involvement in the movement. Kelsey had attended her concert and, when she told me all about her experience, it immediately confirmed my suspicions. I wanted Kelsey to do her school oral on this subject. I wanted to open the eyes of the youth to what was going on behind the scenes and threw myself even deeper into studying the matter.

Kelsey, on the other hand, was not at all interested in doing her class oral on this subject. One Thursday afternoon in late August when I left the office and was heading to the gym, something supernatural happened. I don't care what anybody says, I know the TRUTH – like Jesus always said, *"I tell you the truth"* even though people didn't believe Him. It was as if the enemy wanted to take me out but God had other plans.

I was driving down Boshoff Road towards Victoria Road in Pietermaritzburg when two cars suddenly went straight through a red robot and swerved in front of me. Thankfully I had seen them and managed to avoid a collision. This startled me tremendously and I was very irritated and angry with these dangerous drivers. When I reached Victoria Road, I felt the urge to change lanes and I then moved over into the left lane before heading over the bridge. I looked in my rearview mirror and saw a red car speeding up behind me. It was moving so fast. I could literally see the man's face clearly in my rearview mirror; the car was almost on top of me. I knew it was going to hit me when all of a sudden, the car flipped over, landed on its roof and crash-landed into the lane I had just moved from. I knew right there and then that God had saved my life. He had protected me. I could not believe what I had just witnessed. I was totally stunned at what had just transpired. When I reached the other side of the hill, I rolled down my car window and told the driver in the car next to me that God had just saved my life. With wide eyes, he answered, "And also us!"

God is so POWERFUL – and I truly experienced His protective power over me that day. The way the car flipped over right in my sight I can't explain to others. I guess you had to be there to fully understand how supernatural it was. I have heard of stories before of how supernaturally God's Hand and His angels have protected others in different circumstances and now I believe them. It had now happened to me; Gods angels had protected me.

> **Psalm 91:11**
> *For He shall give His angels charge over you, To keep you in all your ways.*

I tried to tell my book club about the incident that evening and all about *The Illuminati* but none of them were actually very interested. One book club member actually became quite angry and upset with me when I spoke about the evil eye. This is totally understandable as she was not a follower of Christ and she probably thought I was a bit crazy mentioning all these things. Be that as it may, I started bringing Clint's dad's Bible to work and slowly started reading a little bit of the Word. It was the King James Version and quite tricky to understand. I also started listening to a few Christian songs and even started to post some songs on my Facebook feed. I loved Lauren Daigle's music and her influence played a part in bringing me to Christ with her songs *You Say* and *Trust in You*.

Clint and I were invited to the home of our close friends, Chloe and Duane, for dinner. Chloe needed assistance from Clint to do an Airbnb booking online for her upcoming trip to London and Clint had made so many bookings on the site in the past so he was the perfect person to assist her.

It was a cold and misty afternoon in Hilton but Chloe still wanted us to go for a walk before dinner so we could catch up and talk in private while the guys watched rugby on TV. She had a lot on her mind and was feeling confused about her own feelings towards her husband. She mentioned that they were both going for counselling. She wasn't sounding very positive and felt an urge to move to England. I felt so sorry for her and listened as she poured her heart out to me. She stopped twice to pick up feathers in her path and she said, "You probably think I am mad picking up all these feathers." She said she felt they were feathers from her angels. This immediately made me think about the conversation I had had with Sally at *The Bell* in Norfolk a few months earlier and I shared the story with her. I told her that I didn't find it strange at all but rather very intriguing. When we got back to the house, she showed me all the feathers she had collected and relayed some of her stories to me.

That evening she asked me to accompany her to the *Calum Scott* concert in Durban, which was to be held on 9th November 2018. We asked the hubbies if they didn't mind us going and of course they didn't object. Clint then booked accommodation on Airbnb for our girls' night out.

After this visit, I started finding and seeing feathers everywhere. On 29th August 2018, both Chloe and my friend Kobus sent me pictures of a feather they had picked up and held them over their computer keyboards when taking the picture – crazy I know – and what are the chances of them both sending them to me on the same day? This also immediately made me think about Sally and the white feather she had found on her keyboard.

Chloe loved her trip to London. She told me she had asked her angels if she should return to England and leave her husband behind and she said she had specifically asked for a blue feather as a confirmation. On her very last day in the UK, whilst waiting in a school playground for the children her daughter looks after, she said she was amazed by the blue feather she found. Chloe sent me a picture of the blue feather and I had never seen such a beautiful blue feather before. This continued to intrigue me.

A few days past and I went for a walk with Luca, our golden retriever. I had been on a rollercoaster of emotions about whether or not to leave my job, whether to leave the country or not, the typical emotions a lot of South Africans face over unclear futures and that of the future of our children. I boldly stepped out and spoke to my grandfather whom I thought was my guardian angel. I asked him a specific question: "Grandad, if it's the right thing for me to leave my job at the end of next year, please send me a colour feather, but not a white, brown or grey one, a colour one." Kelsey still had one more year of school remaining and I wanted to leave work after that but I was scared and needed confirmation, totally unaware of the dark forces behind the answers you receive. For the remainder of the walk, I looked out for feathers but didn't see any, a little disappointed and deflated, but soon quickly forgot about the question that I had asked.

I hadn't mentioned it to Clint or anyone because, when I mentioned feathers to Clint, he got very irritated and even mocked me one night by shouting, "Feathers are falling everywhere and, yes, Mary-Ann birds shed their feathers."

I also didn't really share too much with him about *The Illuminati* as he could not see it at the time. I recall showing Kelsey and her friend, Brené, old music videos with specific symbolisms in them but didn't really share too much as it was over their heads. I spoke a lot to a colleague about all the events happening as he seemed to understand me and was on the same page as I was.

At the same time, I was still reading the Bible a little at a time and I had found my mom's beautiful wooden Bible that her mom had given her. I posted the song *I Am No Longer a Slave to Fear* on Facebook on 3rd November 2018. I just loved this song. A few days later on 9th November 2018, Chloe and I checked into our lovely Airbnb apartment in Durban, super-excited for the Calum Scott concert. Sipping on a glass of wine, we chatted about our week. I told her a friend of mine, Dave, had popped into the office on the Tuesday and had brought me some green herbs from his garden. He said he drinks weed tea for relaxation before bed as it takes the edge off, especially since he was forced to give up drinking because of liver failure. I had never made the tea and the leaves were thrown out, but I did take along a small bit of weed for Chloe and myself to share.

We shared one small joint, not something I did often, very rarely in actual fact, but I don't want to leave out any detail of the story. It was the first time Chloe had even tried it. We got ready and, when it was time to leave and call the Uber, both our cellphones would not work. Chloe tried three times to call an Uber, something that is so simple to do, but it kept declining her so I tried three times and still it would not allow us to call an Uber. It kept dropping by the payment information. Both quite stressed, we quickly googled how far the Botanical Gardens was and plugged in the location on google maps. As a bonus, it was only a 20-minute walk so we grabbed the cooler box and our deckchairs and set off. We chatted and laughed along the way. Chloe tripped over some garden rubble which had fallen into the broken paving and whilst moaning at me for not warning her, she then dropped her phone which made me look down. As she frantically bent down to pick up her phone, my eyes caught the green feather right in front of me. I was so excited and told Chloe my story about asking my grandad for a colour feather if I should leave work.

We could not stop talking about it and how all the events leading up to picking up the feather was amazing, to the fact that we had to walk and could not catch an Uber. We got to the concert, amazed at what had happened and, after setting up our picnic spot, Chloe looked up the meaning of a green feather. Green is the colour of prosperity, good fortune, abundance and of renewal and growth. "A green feather may be a message of encouragement to move forward with your plans," she said. I saw it as a sign and message from my grandfather that I must move forward and leave my job – it was confirmation and I was so excited about it. We had great fun at the concert and later walked home still amazed at what had transpired.

1 Peter 5:8
Be sober, be vigilant; because your adversary the devil walks about like a roaring lion, seeking whom he may devour.

The next morning on our way back home, Chloe told me all about archangels and I was amazed. I couldn't wait to tell Clint all about our adventure. Clint, always being intrigued by illusion and magic, was now quite captivated as we told him all our feather discoveries, which led him to decide to ask for a blue feather on his early morning run the very next day – bearing in mind that Clint's eyesight is not that great – but I will get to that shortly.

Saturday afternoon was spent on my bed reading all about archangels, Gabriel, Michael, Raphael, and Uriel. I typed in my birthdate on the app and it came up that my angel was Michael, the most powerful angel, I continued to read all about the powers of the different angels. How they speak to us through number plates, colours and other signs. Each angel had different strengths and abilities and I recall reading scriptures in the Bible about them too. However, God never intended us to commune with angels but only with Him.

I clearly recall, that night, asking Archangel Raphael to help me with Kelsey's healing and to show me how I could assist her. I also asked for specific feathers – a purple feather whether to move to London, a yellow feather whether to move to New Zealand or a pink feather whether to stay in South Africa.

Waking up on the Sunday morning, the first thing I noticed whilst walking down the passage was a purple bottle on the ledge. It was a bottle of tissue salts and no-one knew who put it there or how it had gotten there, and it was a strange location for it to be in the first place.

Clint was on his usual morning run with Luca and, when he returned, he put a tiny blue feather under the purple bottle which was on the ledge. Clint had clearly been quite fascinated by all the feather stories from the previous day, which led to him asking for a blue feather on his early morning run. I am not 100% sure what the exact question was that he had asked but, when asking him months later who he had actually asked for the feather, he said he had asked God. Clint's eyesight is not that great at all; he barely recognises people in the shopping centres or in the street without his glasses on. He relayed the story to us as we sat under the lapa. He said that, after asking for the blue feather, his eyes were drawn to feathers and blue objects en route, but saw no sign of a blue feather. Then, when he was just a few metres from our home, he said that in the road – he couldn't believe it – his eyes were drawn to this tiny feather, the size of a small coin and, when he bent down to pick it up, he was shocked and blown away that it was a beautiful tiny bright blue feather. He quickly went into the house and returned with the feather to show us. I was in shock. A feather like that you just don't see lying in the streets.

I told him about the tissue salts and my requests from the previous night – the request for Kelsey's healing and the request about moving. It was then when he told me that was where he had put the feather, the minute he walked in the door, and wondered where this bottle had come from. I looked up tissues salts that would help Kelsey's condition and read that variants 14 and 25 would be good but one needed a doctor's prescription to get them. I never did get those tissue salts and now we pray for healing from the great Physician, Jehovah-Rapha, and we eagerly wait for that miracle.

Luke 8:50
But when Jesus heard it, He answered him saying, "Do not be afraid; only believe, and she will be made well."

Chapter 4

Spiritual Warfare

Day-to-day details of events and accounts that took place from the 12th of November to the 26th of November 2018 (The intense period of our spiritual warfare).

12th November 2018 – Monday

We woke up early to find that our geyser in the house had burst. Clint called the insurance company and I rushed off to work super-excited to tell my work colleagues, Angela and Kobus, all about the concert, feathers and archangels. I looked up their archangels wherein it indicated they both had the same one – Gabriel. My mom's archangel was also Gabriel. I typed in my birthday again that morning and I was very disappointed that now all of a sudden, my archangel was Uriel. I kept punching in my birthdate but it kept showing 'Uriel'. It was strange how, on Saturday at home, it indicated 'Michael'. Angela then showed me an angel book that she had at work and spoke to me about Ethan, her husband, being a man of God. I called Kobus and relayed all the stories to him. I think he started to worry about all the talk of feathers and archangels and he told me that I could give my life to the Lord at any time and in any place. He said one did not have to be in a church to do that.

Romans 10:13
For whoever calls on the name of the Lord shall be saved.

Those few words changed my life forever and I will always be grateful for my friend's counsel and guidance. I left work at 3:30 pm to go for my usual tennis elbow therapy with my physio, Des, and as I left, I saw a truck with loads of workers on the back all wearing lumo green uniforms. I recalled that archangels speak to you in colours and different things. I wondered what it meant.

When I arrived at Victoria Road, I saw a car with the number plate 'Uriel' (my archangel). I was shocked and I thought I was seeing things. I decided there and then to give my life to the Lord. I asked God to come into my life that afternoon. I was alone in my car. God knows what's in your heart and He knew I meant it.

Even though at that stage I did not even understand that Jesus was actually God and that I was so messed up with all the feathers and archangels, total confusion as to what the truth was, He knew I meant the God of the Bible, the God of Abraham, Isaac and Jacob.

I shared all my stories with Des about the signs and wonders and all my experiences I had had over the past few days.

Jeremiah 29:13
And you will seek Me and find Me, when you search for Me with all your heart.

I arrived home to a huge mess – a massive hole in our celling where they had removed the geyser. I was annoyed with this as previously they had always gone through the roof, but not this time. That night, Clint and I were lying in Kelsey's room whilst she was studying for her exams. She loves company and enjoyed us just being there with her.

I then asked Clint, out of the blue, what he was looking at on his phone – something which I don't usually do but Clint had an intense look about him. He told me he had just logged on to LinkedIn and this image had appeared on his feed which he found strange. He took a screen shot and sent it to me. It was of a feather and the message read, *"You've got a new story to write. And it looks nothing like your past."*

That same night, Angela sent me a picture of her daughter wearing a bright purple baby outfit. Lumo colours, numbers and other signs played a big role over the next few days. Earlier that day she had also shown me a picture of Ethan, her husband, and a small speck of lumo green caught my eye which she said she had also noticed.

13 November 2018 – Tuesday

I woke up with terrible stomach pain so I didn't go to work. We had a gentleman by the name of Ali who came that morning to chop down a tree at the bottom of our garden. I sat outside by the pool and I was amazed at how happy I actually felt and how at peace I was.

I was watching a dragonfly and felt like I was being spiritually awakened. It's hard to explain. I called Chloe and told her all about it. I told her something was happening to me and that I was so happy. She said she had also seen a dragonfly that morning but that she wasn't really in a great place and she really wished that she could feel as happy as I was that day. I felt really bad for her. We have been friends for years and it broke my heart to see a once happy family now falling apart.

I didn't know what I could do for either of them as they were both going through such a difficult and rough stage in their lives. I thought about Duane and how his heart was breaking. I sent him a beautiful Christian song called *Start Over* by Flame and I told him everything would work out; that he must just put his trust in God.

I also called another friend in my excitement and asked him if there was a number plate with 'Uriel' or if I had imagined this. He confirmed that there was a personalised number plate like this and that it was indeed registered in Pietermaritzburg.

I then called Kobus and told him I felt like I was on a spiritual journey and that I had taken his advice and given my life to God. Even though I struggled that day with terrible uterus pains, I couldn't help but feel joy in my heart. I felt so different.

14 November 2018 – Wednesday

I still wasn't feeling great when I woke up, so I stayed at home again. Kelsey was also at home as she was studying for exams. Ali arrived early that morning to collect some rubble from the side of our garage as well as parts of the tree he had chopped down the previous day. I went out to greet him and he wanted to speak to me. He told me of a very strange experience he had encountered when he left our house the previous day. As he had left, he saw a bright green snake in the middle of the road. He looked over the wall at my neighbour's garden in an attempt to describe the shade of green. It was a very bright green and the snake had stood up like a cobra in the middle of the road, looking straight at him. He couldn't believe what he was seeing because it wasn't a cobra, yet it stood up like one. He had watched the snake and then it slithered towards the grass and stood up again in a striking position, looking straight at him before sliding up into a tree. He said he should have killed it.

I rushed indoors and immediately looked up the meaning of a snake in a striking pose. I read that snakes represent a sign of change, a spiritual awakening, a transition period and fertility.

At the time I thought Ali's message was a positive one, so I went back outside to tell him and thank him. He told me he had no idea why he had relayed this story to me but that he had found the incident extremely strange. I could see in his eyes that he didn't think this was a good sign, but he was glad I was happy about it.

While I was standing there chatting to him, my eyes caught sight of the dog's tennis ball right at the end of the area where they were clearing all the rubble. As I approached the fence to pick up the ball, I saw a beautiful big clean white feather as white as snow. It was strange to see such a clean feather as the entire area had become such a mess with dust and sand blowing everywhere from all the rubble. I went inside to show Kelsey the feather and she told me it looked just like a real angel feather.

I called my mom to tell her the story about the snake and I wasn't going to mention a word about the feather and all about her archangel, Gabriel, but I couldn't help myself. My mom's favourite number was 13 and that was also Gabriel's number. I laughed when telling her about her archangel, Gabriel, because I said he likes to communicate through the phone and I was phoning her, telling her all about him. I told her I was on a spiritual journey. I don't think she was too sure of what to make of it all.

Feeling a lot better, I went to dinner with the girls that night.

Someone in the restaurant was taking many pictures as there were many flashes of light. I then thought about the archangels again.

Clint was at an annual supplier's event in Durban that evening and was staying over. He said he didn't know what had come over him that night but he was telling all the guys at the table that marriage was not something he would want his girls to be involved in. He said it's much better to remain single and not waste money on weddings. He also had strong views on having a man cave. He was really putting forward strong, harsh words against the principles of marriage. We had not been sleeping in the same bed for some time because of his constant snoring and he would be up the whole night playing chess online and watching tennis. I would go to bed earlyish. He called me from the function that evening for us to listen to the Muslim prayer. I had no idea why he had done that.

That night, I asked for healing in my uterus. I awoke in the early hours of the morning with the most excruciating stomach pain. I lay in agony for quite some time. Then I felt a warm rush, a strange feeling and then all the pain was gone. It was weird and it felt as though I had been healed.

15 November 2018 – Thursday

Whilst travelling to work that morning, the first thing I heard was the news on East Coast Radio and thereafter the presenters were talking about a famous movie star who had died – Kim Porter. Thereafter they played the song called *The Sound of Silence* by Disturbed. I cranked up the volume. The lyrics actually mention neon gods. It is actually a disturbing song but I was singing it at the top of my lungs. It seemed to energise me.

I had already been drawn to neon and lumo colours because of what I had read on 'google' with regard to how the archangels speak to us, specifically through colours, light and number plates. After the song finished, the presenter spoke abount a fortune-teller and a prank call that she had made to a lady, speaking about someone dying at three o'clock in the morning. I remember the whole story disturbed me and I felt really sorry for the lady they had played a prank on.

I parked my car and saw a dragonfly hovering around. I walked to my office and, by the time I arrived, I was in tears and very emotional. I told Angela about the warm sensation I had experienced after asking the archangel for healing. I also relayed the stories of the past few days. I had begun to experience spiritual warfare and I was not prepared for what lay ahead over the next few days.

A friend of mine, Patrick, had popped in for coffee and a quick chat. He had noticed the Bible on my desk and asked me about it. He had just picked it up when Clint phoned to speak to me. They then spoke briefly to greet each other and discussed the only verse in the Bible that Patrick knew – John 3:16: *"For God so loved the world that He gave His only begotten Son, that whoever believes in Him should not perish but have everlasting life."* Clint knew this verse and relayed it back to Patrick who told Clint he was shocked that I was reading the Bible. Clint told Patrick he had no idea that I even had a Bible at work and was reading it. They both had a chuckle and finished the call.

Later that same day, three very strange events happened, one after the other.

1. At around lunch time, out of the blue, Angela sent me a picture of a random man in his paramedic

green uniform – the symbol of Archangel Raphael. Angela even told me much later that she had no idea why she sent it to me. She was just standing around waiting to buy food.

2. One of Sharné's friends' mother, Belinda, called me straight thereafter. She never phones me but had called to discuss the safety of our girls. She relayed the story of the man who had just been murdered around the corner from where we stay. She was talking so softly that I could barely hear what she was trying to tell me. There was real fear and worry in her voice.

3. As I put down the phone, Patrick called to say that a bird had just flown into his office with a pink feather in its beak. Whilst he was still on the phone talking to me, I just burst out crying and I had the most terrifying thought that my mother was dying and that she was not saved.

Patrick had no idea that I had even asked for a pink feather. He also didn't have a clue why I was crying and I just put the phone down.

Sudden FEAR gripped me like never before. I was sobbing and totally distraught. Three ladies came into my office to pray for me. I don't think they had ever seen me like that before. They mainly prayed in isiZulu so I wasn't too sure of what they were saying but I knew I needed prayer cover. The one lady who works downstairs said she had no idea why she had even come to my office that afternoon as she had no reason to do so and didn't need anything from me.

How great is our God that He sends people into our lives at

just the right time to pray for us.

As I left my office, I saw a small white feather at the door which triggered more fear and tears and I knew I had to see my mom. The spirit world is real – very real – I just didn't know it at the time. There was a war raging in my mind. Demon spirits are real and it's terrifying.

1 Timothy 4:1
Now the Spirit expressly says that in latter times some will depart from the faith, giving heed to deceiving spirits and doctrines of demons.

I was nearly home when I had a sudden urge to visit my mom in Howick – a 30-minute drive from Pietermaritzburg. I called Clint and the girls to tell them I was going to see her. I was very upset and shaken and I said that, if anything should happen to me, they must know that I love them. This was very upsetting for them as I had never done anything like that before and I had no idea why I even said it. I just knew there was an urgency to get to my mom and there was a big storm brewing.

I knew I had to get there fast. On my drive to my mom, I recall seeing an ambulance with the same green paramedic uniformed men that Angela had sent to me earlier that day. There was also a lot of lightening and I was petrified. I had never in my life felt like this. I begged God to please just let me see my mother before she died. I was convinced she was dying and that she would be dead by the time I got there.

I thought Archangel Uriel was speaking to me through the constant flashes of lightening and that Archangel Gabriel was trying to tell me something of great urgency. The more the lightning and thunder occurred, the more petrified I became and the faster I drove to get there.

This is not of the Lord and a bigger storm was brewing in me. The enemy, knowing full well that I was growing closer to the real God (Jesus) and that the enemy's time was coming to an end, he was trying his best to keep me from my destiny and finding the way.

> **John 10:10**
> *The thief does not come except to steal, and to kill, and to destroy. I have come that they may have life, and that they may have it more abundantly.*

When I got to my mom's place, I was relieved to see that she was perfectly fine and in good health.

I needed to tell her that she had to be saved, that Jesus is the only way to Heaven and that she had to be born again – a scripture which I had highlighted in her old wooden Bible.

> **John 3:3**
> *Jesus answered and said to him, "Most assuredly, I say to you, unless one is born again, he cannot see the kingdom of God."*

I did not know how to approach the subject as my mom was not a practising Christian and a very private person when it came to her faith. She told Clint and myself that we should not speak about politics or religion and often told us to keep it inside.

I told her my memory was getting really bad and I needed her to pray for me, thinking this would perhaps ignite her to speak about God and a mother will do anything for her children. I thought she would be open to prayer in order to help me and thereby build her own relationship with God.

She had been a practising Christian many years prior. However, after becoming a biology teacher, she was blinded by the enemy and started being deceived to the notion of evolution and soon thereafter became an atheist.

I told her that I had given my life to the Lord and I tried to plant a few seeds. I asked if I could pray with her which she agreed to and thereafter, I drove back home.

> **Acts 2:36**
> *Therefore let all the house of Israel know assuredly that God has made this Jesus, whom you crucified, both Lord and Christ.*

16 November 2018 – Friday

I excitedly sent messages to my brother and sisters informing them I had prayed with our mom and that I had told her she needed to be saved in order to go to Heaven. I sent my sister, Linda, in Australia, pictures of highlighted verses from the Bible and told her that I had given my life to God.

I found two receipts in my office desk drawer that morning. I thought this was peculiar and wondered where they had come from. I noticed they had Dave's name on them and he had been to visit me in my office the week before. I studied the receipts, noticing he had paid R50 for a pineapple which reflected on the one receipt and on the other one it reflected he had paid R60 for a lettuce. He had only bought those two items at two different shops. I was shocked at why he would pay so much money for these items so I called him. He wondered how his slips had landed up in my drawer and told me it was R50 for a box of pineapples and R60 for a box of lettuce. I still found it odd as he lives on his own. Why he would buy a box of each item? We had a good laugh and a quick chat before saying our goodbyes.

Even though he had retired, he still popped in every now and again for a quick visit and a cup of coffee. Over the years, we had built a wonderful friendship. He now resides in England and we still catch up at least once a month for updates. Secretly, I am waiting for the Lord to work in his life, to soften his heart and open his eyes. I am eagerly awaiting his salvation.

That night we had a braai *(barbeque)*. Clint and I were chatting outside. He was telling me all about the supplier's function which he had attended and how there was discussion sparked around the table, when the salad was being passed around, specifically on pineapple and lettuce, I was surprised that the same two items that Clint was now talking about were the items on the receipts I had found. I rushed to my handbag and quickly retrieved them. I showed them to Clint and told him I had found them in my desk drawer earlier that day and that I had actually called Dave to ask him about the prices of the pineapple and lettuce. We were both baffled at what it meant and found it to be a bizarre coincidence.

Clint had also received a call out of the blue from an old colleague from his days when he worked at Simba and he had invited us to a braai in Hilton. The colleague, whom Clint had not seen in 20 years, said he was moving to a new house and he told Clint not to bring any meat because he had so much meat that he needed to braai and he wanted to cook it all. Clint didn't have the heart to tell him that I had just given up meat a day or two before, as I had told Clint that God had created everything and I didn't want to eat God's creation anymore.

The enemy had planted that seed in my head, as God gave us everything to eat. Nevertheless, Clint agreed that we would go and found it so strange that Ryan had called him out of the blue. However, we were super-excited to catch up with them after so many years.

Genesis 9:3
Every moving thing that lives shall be food for you. I have given you all things, even as the green herbs.

1 Timothy 4:4-5
[4]For every creature of God is good, and nothing is to be refused if it is received with thanksgiving; [5]for it is sanctified by the word of God and prayer.

We went to bed relatively early as Clint had to go to Durban the next morning and I had to take Sharné to a market in Howick. She had been asked by some stranger in a shop, whilst working as a promoter for a chocolate company, if she would please help the man's wife who needed assistance selling cream.

He wanted to fetch Sharné on that Saturday morning but we refused. We were not sure who this man was so we agreed that I would rather take her to the market myself. I had discussed with my mom that I would come to visit her and we could both go to the market together.

17 November 2018 – Saturday

We were all up early. Clint arranged for a lift to Durban to collect a vehicle and Sharné and I headed for the farmer's market in Howick.

I met the lady that Sharné was going to work for. She had

a speech impediment and we had thought she would be selling fresh cream but it was actually hand and body cream. She had a lovely stall and the whole market was in an old farm barn.

When I left the barn, I saw a lot of white feathers lying on the ground and by the time I arrived at my mom's house, I was frantic!! I told my mom I had dropped off Sharné, I didn't know who the lady was and I didn't have her contact details. Sharné didn't have her phone with her and I needed to get back there as fast as possible. I cannot explain the fear that gripped me and I felt like something terrible was going to happen to her.

My poor mom rushed out of her house, clean forgetting her walking stick and off we sped to the market. My mom was worried about me and said that alcohol had made my dad go mad and now it was making me go crazy, remembering that I had rushed there on Thursday in a panic.

I told her that it wasn't the alcohol but that I would never drink again if she agreed to give her life to the Lord.

She said she would and I said I wouldn't drink again. I didn't touch a drop of alcohol until months later when Clint said that my mom hadn't really given her life to the Lord. However, to this day, I have never been drunk again. Thank you, Jesus, for delivering me from this terrible addiction of alcohol.

> **1 Corinthians 6:9-11**
> *⁹Do you not know that the unrighteous will not inherit the kingdom of God? Do not be deceived. Neither fornicators, nor idolaters, nor adulterers, nor homosexuals, nor sodomites, ¹⁰nor thieves, nor covetous, nor drunkards, nor revilers, nor extortioners will inherit the kingdom of God. ¹¹And*

such were some of you. But you were washed, but you were sanctified, but you were justified in the name of the Lord Jesus and by the Spirit of our God.

When I walked in and saw Sharné working, selling the creams, my heart was at peace and I instantly calmed down. I spoke to Kirsty whom I now had been properly introduced to. We chatted about her daughter and how she had travelled the world trying to find products to help her daughter's skin condition. She gave me a complimentary bottle of the cream and I also purchased a bottle. The cream was called 'Nourish' and it smelt beautiful.

My mom bought some veggies and we sat down while I ate a charcoal roll with a veggie burger patty as I no longer ate meat.

I recall us laughing because there were so many elderly people with their dogs there that morning and we thought about her mom (my granny) who loved her dog Zola, named after Zola Budd, a famous South African runner.

My mom, on the other hand, was not fond of dogs or pets in general. I think over the years her four children put her off pets, always bringing them home and then leaving them in her hands to take care of.

While I was still eating, Clint called me. He was travelling back from Durban and I went outside to take the call as it was hard to hear him in the noisy barn. I picked up a 10-cent piece whilst on the phone with him and put it in my pocket.

I left my mom leaning against a wall at the barns entrance as she didn't have her walking stick with her and I quickly went to say goodbye to Sharné and Kirsty. When I returned to my mom, the first thing I noticed was a ring of white feathers all around my mom's feet.

I knew the angels were protecting her and that God was watching over her and relieved that she had committed her life to God; well, so I thought at the time.

Little did I know that she had told Sharné at the market she had just said that in order to please me and in the hope of me not ever drinking again.

That afternoon, I picked up Sharné and chatted to Kirsty once again as she packed her things into her car. I told her I was on a spiritual journey and she said that her husband had been a pastor.

I asked her about a scripture that a colleague at work had told me of a few days prior. I said I couldn't find it in the Bible and it had disturbed me.

It was about a rich man throwing money down from heaven to the people. She said she would ask her husband and would call me. I never did get that call but months later I realised that the story was actually about God throwing down manna from heaven and not money. It was the story of how God had taken the Israelites out of captivity in slavery and it was when they were in the desert for 40 years that God gave them manna from heaven.

Exodus 16:4
Then the LORD said to Moses, "Behold, I will rain bread from heaven for you. And the people shall go out and gather a certain quota every day, that I may test them, whether they will walk in My law or not.

John 6:31-35
³¹Our fathers ate the manna in the desert; as it is written, 'He gave them bread from heaven to eat.' ³²Then Jesus said to them, "Most assuredly, I say to you, Moses did not give you the bread from heaven, but My Father gives you the true bread from heaven. ³³For the bread of God is He who comes down from heaven and gives life to the world." ³⁴Then they said to Him, "Lord, give us this bread always." ³⁵And Jesus said to them, "I am the bread of life. He who comes to Me shall never hunger, and he who believes in Me shall never thirst."

We headed back to my mom's as Sharné said she wanted to say goodbye to her as she was going to Australia on the 25th of November and wouldn't get a chance to come back to Howick.

When we drove into Amber Valley, the security guard, who was wearing a Knight's Security uniform, said to us "Oh, I see there's going to be a big party tonight!" I told him definitely not at my mom's house, that was for sure and Sharné and I had a good laugh. Sharné said her goodbyes and we headed home.

When we reached home, I had a long hot shower. I felt excited, yet nervous. I heard loud drums and music – African music. The family across the road were having a huge party. They seldom have functions and I had never heard such drumming coming from their house and we have never again since.

I told Clint that we should be going there and not to his friend's house. I said God was telling us to go there but he said I was being silly and we were going to the braai at Ryan's house in Hilton.

I was thinking about the security guard mentioning the huge party and felt drawn to the house across the road.

I also told Clint that I had found a ten-cent piece earlier that day at the market when I was on the phone with him and he told me that the only item in the car that he had collected that morning was a ten-cent piece in the driver's side panel.

He also then told me out of the blue he knew the song I wanted to tell him about from Thursday. I couldn't remember and it had been bugging me. He said it was called *The Sound of Silence* by Disturbed.

I was blown away at how he knew this and quickly ran down the passage to the study to play the song on the desktop computer. I called Clint and played it for him and he said it was a disturbing song.

When we left for the braai, there were loads of cars all over the street. Clint nearly bumped into one of them and I was still not too sure about why I was feeling so drawn to go to that party across the road. It was the seed that the security guard had planted in my mind but we continued to the braai in Hilton. Clint said I was being ridiculous and we needed to go to Ryan's house as agreed.

We arrived at Ryans house and the first thing I noticed was the Knight's security guard sign. I felt a bit uneasy but the feeling faded away quickly.

I had just that very morning given up drinking so I had soda water and Clint had a glass of wine. Donvae commented on the dandelion on the wine bottle and told us her business cards had a dandelion on them as well.

She said, "When you look at it, just breathe"; another

peculiar incident as Kelsey's room has a dandelion painting on the wall with the words 'Just Breathe' on it, a painting she had done.

We sat outside looking at the beautiful view. It was a misty cool evening. We chatted about our work and places we had been to on holiday. We had both been to Mabibi (Thonga Beach Lodge) and agreed that it was a fantastic destination for snorkelling.

Their son told me that he remembered killing all the mosquitoes there. I had been arguing strongly with Clint telling him that we can't kill anything as God created everything. He had said we can kill certain things like drain flies in the shower and at that moment I felt it was okay to also kill mosquitoes. I know this sounds crazy but everything that happened to me and Clint over the next few days was crazy.

My senses had been so heightened that evening. Something so supernatural was happening that it is very hard to explain and put into words. Donvae showed me all her beautiful mosaic work and chairs that each member of the family had made. I was sitting on the yin and yang mosaic chair. The doorbell rang and another couple arrived – Olga and her husband, Rod, and their children.

We were not informed that anyone else had been invited and I was instantly intrigued by Olga. It seemed like we had a lot in common. We had the same number of sisters and she also had a brother. Her one sister was also living in Australia as did mine. She spoke a lot about Graaff-Reinet, a place where I attended junior school, and a place nearby called *The Barn Owl* (a place where water will apparently never run out.) She mentioned that I must play the lotto – I started feeling like she was a fortune-teller of sorts and I started to feel uneasy.

They were talking about killing rats and then feeling sorry for them. The conversation had my mind spinning and it was very confusing to me.

Clint was chatting to Ryan and Rod. Rod was telling Clint all about magic and Clint told them all about a popular illusionist and magician he had recently met named Harry. He had attended a golf day in August and was captivated by Harry, the magician. His show had left Clint gobsmacked and the following day, whilst sitting at breakfast with his colleague Patrick, Harry asked Clint what had impressed him most about his show the previous night. He had said it was the way in which he read people's minds. He told Clint to think of anything and to type it into google search on his phone. Harry was a few meters away from Clint so there would have been no way for Harry to have the faintest clue of what Clint was looking up and typing on his phone.

Clint typed in 'Roger Federer' on his phone. Harry then requested that he place the phone face down on the table in front of them and then get up and approach him. Harry then looked deep into his eyes and asked him if it was a sportsperson, to which Clint agreed. He then asked if it was a South African sportsperson to which Clint replied "He could be" as Roger's mom (Lynette) is a South African. Then Harry said he needed to touch him and he placed his hand on Clint's shoulder. Again, he looked deep into his eyes. Harry said, "Roger Federer" and winked at him. This blew Clint's mind. He was so astounded about how Harry had done this and told everyone he knew about it. He even tried to convince his superiors to organise for Harry to attend their annual conference.

Clint said the way Harry looked at him was very disturbing,

deep and rather intense. It was piercing as though he had looked right into his soul.

Clint's love for magic and illusion from an early age would play out over the next few days. The transferring of spirits is very real.

Clint also had an absolute obsession for his favourite tennis star, Roger Federer. I can honestly say that Roger was Clint's idol. There would not be a tennis match that Clint would miss out on and he would know Roger's every move. Clint worshipped him.

We had on numerous occasions travelled to Dubai to watch Roger play tennis and we have had the privilege of meeting him personally. Clint went to Dubai for seven consecutive years to watch the tennis tournament.

Clint today still loves his tennis and his favourite player remains Roger Federer but he is no longer his idol.

I went to the bathroom and saw a paper plane lying in the passage. This triggered an emotion about my mom. We had entered a competition a few weeks prior where we had made paper planes together and we went to her house to fly them. Sharné had my 84-year-old mother and me rushing down the banks at Amber Valley trying to get the planes to fly. We had a few good laughs with our many failed attempts whilst my poor mom was holding onto her walking stick.

I was then instantly gripped by fear and was again paranoid that my mom had died. I had to call her immediately. I was so relieved to hear her voice on the other end of the line and just said I was checking to see if everything was okay.

We had dinner and watched the rugby. South Africa was playing Scotland in a test match. Everything on the TV was so green. The grass on the rugby field was literally popping out at me. My senses were on a sharp knife-edge and so heightened. I was feeling really uneasy and I felt like everyone was watching me to see what I was going to do. I was uncertain about everything – what I should eat and what I shouldn't eat. I remember squeezing Clint's arm, begging him to take me home. I told him something was very wrong I was not myself. I was extremely anxious about being there.

We left halfway through the game. When Donvae said goodbye to us at the door, she was holding the paper plane and I asked her if I could take it with me. They must have thought we were so rude but I had to get out of there fast. The girls were really surprised to see us home so early.

Clint and I were up the whole night talking about God. In the early hours of the morning, I was convinced we needed to write a book for new Christians to make it simpler as the Bible 'is so difficult to understand and such a hard read'. That was the spirit of deception coming in as the Bible is the true living Word of God, which the enemy likes to keep us out of by all means possible.

The Bible is the way in which we develop an intimate relationship with Jesus Christ. It's the way we grow and develop in His knowledge. His Word is a lamp to our feet and food for our soul. It's the Word that we need to fight the enemy with.

Psalm 119:105
Your Word is a lamp to my feet and a light to my path.

Unbeknown to me, I was being manipulated in the spirit realm, making me believe that we needed to write a new book. Clint and I were being totally deceived and at this stage we were not fully aware of the demonic attack of deception and lies from the devil.

> **Revelation 22:18-19**
> [18]*For I testify to everyone who hears the words of the prophecy of this book: If anyone adds to these things, God will add to him the plagues that are written in this book;* [19]*and if anyone takes away from the words of the book of this prophecy, God shall take away his part from the Book of Life, from the holy city, and from the things which are written in this book.*

I was convinced that we needed to make starter packs for new believers like ourselves with our new book and some songs.

We spoke about the ten-cent pieces we had both found earlier that day and I said it must be all about the 10 Commandments. Sleep became a thing of the past.

18 November 2018 – Sunday

Clint and I both went for a walk around the block early Sunday morning. We were both crying – sobbing. They were tears of sheer joy. We were both seeing the beauty of God's creation for what felt like the very first time. We had never seen things the way we were seeing them now – absolute beauty – everything was so clear and I asked Clint how anyone who ever saw what we were seeing could ever turn their backs on God. The grass, flowers, birds, insects, feathers and sky were all so bright and it was just wonderful – euphoric.

It was as if our eyes had been closed for all these years and we were only now on this very day getting to experience the sheer beauty of life itself. Everything was alive. It was a supernatural experience hard to put into words. We spoke the entire day about God and it felt like His angels were in heaven typing out everything we were saying for this book that God wanted us to write.

Little did I know it was this book that God had intended me to write.

Clint said he felt he had now been shifted into the spiritual realm. He was experiencing things on a different level. He said it felt as if he had moved into a different dimension, totally different to anything he had ever experienced before in his life. He felt different as if he was no longer on earth and over the next few days this strange sensation intensified. The momentary visions he received were both intriguing and terrifying.

That evening we needed to understand what was going on with us, so we went to visit our friends, Phil and Charmaine Gill, whom we knew have been Christians for many years. We were both unsure whether to go or not. There was an uneasiness in us. It didn't feel safe for us to leave but we had so many questions that we needed answers to.

There was a car parked in our driveway, belonging to someone visiting our neighbours. It was as if it was preventing us from going. We asked them to move and then headed to the Gills.

I told them all about giving my life to the Lord and then of the total fear of my mom dying. They said it was spiritual warfare, but we did not really understand it at that stage.

They were so happy for us and gave us a few Christian CD's, a New Testament Bible and Charmaine gave us a box of herbal tea.

Their home was so warm and inviting, filled with so many scripture verses. We left feeling a bit more at ease and later listened to the CD's. Clint continued to play those CD's morning, noon and night.

We got very little sleep that night and I was woken up at 3 am yet again with the terrible fear that my mom had died. I begged Clint to call as I couldn't face her not answering. We sat up together talking nonstop about God until it was a reasonable time to call my mom. She answered the phone and I was relieved.

19 November 2018 – Monday

I called my boss first thing on Monday morning and told him that I would not be able to make it to work as I was on a spiritual journey and that he would understand. He had just lost his dad and was on compassionate leave.

I told him I would explain everything when I got back to work. He said, "But, Mary-Ann, you're on leave from next week as you're going to London." I told him I knew that but I wouldn't be able to come to work. I hadn't slept properly now for two nights. I felt totally different.

Terror and fear gripped me once again. It felt like my life was crashing around me, as if I was breaking and shattering into a thousand pieces. I wouldn't wish this feeling on anyone.

As I sat at the dining room table that morning, my eyes were drawn to Kelsey's grade 11 art book and, as I started looking through it, I had the intense feeling that Kelsey was going to die. I started screaming for Ntombi, our domestic worker, to pray for me.

It felt like something was attacking my stomach, making me feel so sick. That feeling only subsided after she prayed.

I could feel the attack returning. This would come in waves and I would call for Ntombi to pray for me again. This went on for the entire day.

Ntombi had never seen me like this before. We are so blessed that she is a Christian; a child of God. She said she knew demons were tormenting me, but she had never in the 16 years of working for us experienced anything like this.

It was so strange because on the one hand I was seeing such beauty and on the other I was gripped by fear and paranoia.

It felt as if Kelsey's art book was coming alive and I was walking through her life. The next few days were crazy. We survived on very little sleep and practically no food. I couldn't eat. I had sores all over my mouth. I could not function properly and the feeling in the pit of my stomach was not going away.

I kept waking up at 3 am every morning looking at the clock with the fear that someone had died. I would look at our coffee mugs and be reminded of someone. I would burst into tears thinking the person had died.

It was so real and even Clint said that during this time he looked at objects in our home differently, as if they were carrying a secret message, codes, revealing things to us. They were planting seeds in our thoughts; planting fear and doubt into our minds.

I found it difficult that day to move away from Kelsey's art book. I sobbed thinking she was dying and the seed was planted in my head about the Oscars because she had recently done an incredible art project on the Oscars.

Over the next few days, I was so confused as to what was going on, I felt as though I was constantly being watched and monitored in my every move. It felt as if I was in a real live movie and God and His angels were watching me from heaven.

It was as if I had to complete certain tasks set before me but that I was constantly failing God and not being able to complete anything and at times not even being able to recall what the tasks actually were. It truly felt as though I had to save the earth from destruction and that the tasks or assignments were tests given to me daily by God but I was not worthy and unable to complete the assignment. Each day I would be derailed, sobbing, believing I failed God.

Clint had sent me a WhatsApp message that read: "We on a powerful journey here I'm getting messages from God to guide us, Kelsey is terrified the pace is too quick she's scared, I looked at my phone and this image tells the story we must keep going but don't flood like this, we need daily bread not all day bread, we will just stay focused its slow, scary, exciting but it's real, it's a marathon I love you to bits we are all together on this journey please pray to ease your mind but keep you focused."

Clint and I were both caught up in terrible spiritual warfare. Two ordinary people having a supernatural encounter at the same time? When I look back now and think of the feeling of failing God and being mortified that I had not gotten the task right, yet every day He would forgive me and I would try again, it reminds me of how God's mercies are new every day. He is forgiving and if we get it wrong, His Word reminds us that He will never leave us nor forsake us.

> **Hebrews 13:5**
> *Let your conduct be without covetousness; be content with such things as you have. For He Himself has said, "I will never leave you nor forsake you."*
>
> **Lamentations 3:22-24**
> *[22] Through the Lord's mercies we are not consumed, Because His compassions fail not. [23] They are new every morning; Great is Your faithfulness. [24] "The Lord is my portion," says my soul, "Therefore I hope in Him!"*

I called my brother that evening telling him something was terribly wrong. I told him I had given my life to the Lord and that this was happening because I didn't know the Bible.

I told him I was being tormented and hadn't slept in a few days. I recall him clearly shouting over the telephone, "There are no demons, get back to earth, man!" David was really quite shaken by what was going on and he didn't know how to deal with it. He was really worried about me and being so far away, as he lives in the Cape, he had no idea what was going on with us.

Wendy, his wife, told me months later that David wanted to come and help us, but she had advised against it as she told him he was not equipped to deal with this sort of thing.

John Hagee, an international renowned author and pastor, had been in the ministry for a few years before he encountered a woman, Mrs Smith, possessed with a demon. He said he had not been prepared at all for what he encountered. Very few people in the ministry are equipped to deal with spiritual, demonic activity. He describes this in detail in his book called *The Three Heavens*.

I knew there was something terribly wrong and the terror I was experiencing was not of God.

I do, however, believe that God allowed this all to happen to us for our own good. He allowed me to be on the threshing floor – I needed it – turning both our lives around.

All I know is that I wanted a pastor and I needed help desperately. I asked my brother to send a pastor.

> **Hebrews 12:11**
> *Now no chastening seems to be joyful for the present, but painful; nevertheless, afterward it yields the peaceable fruit of righteousness to those who have been trained by it.*

20 November 2018 – Tuesday

We both didn't get much sleep yet again. Overwhelmed by our emotions, we realised that we were in need of help.

I called Angela, my colleague, first thing in the morning, asking her to please ask her husband, Ethan, to come and pray for us. I recalled her telling me a few days earlier that Ethan was a strong Christian with a calling on his life to preach.

I told her something was going on and we needed prayer and a pastor to teach us about the Bible. I really believed that this was happening to us because I didn't have a good solid understanding on the Word of God and I did not know much about the Bible besides basic Bible stories taught at Sunday school. As I mentioned earlier, I did not have the understanding of Jesus being God at that time. However, we must never forget that God is all knowing and knows what's in our hearts. What He ultimately looks at is our hearts.

> **Psalm 51:10**
> *Create in me a clean heart, O God, And renew a steadfast spirit within me.*

Angela said she would rather ask her pastor, Jonathan, to come to our house. She could hear in my voice over the phone that I was desperate and she urgently requested her pastor to pay us a visit. Soon thereafter, Pastor Jonathan arrived at our home. He had a fantastic knowledge of the Bible and gave us some scriptures. He spoke very well, calmly relaying stories of how he had travelled the world preaching the gospel.

The lack of sleep over the past few nights was now taking its toll on us and we found it extremely difficult to understand and follow everything Pastor Jonathan was relaying to us. However, when he left, we said that God had sent the right man and we were very grateful that he had come to our home.

I am not sure what he thought of the situation or what he thought was going on at the time, but months later, Pastor Jonathan said he felt that on his first visit I had something demonic in me and on his second visit he felt that it was in Clint.

Clint had told my brother, David, via a text message, that we were working through everything and that we were exhausted. He asked him to pray for us but not to send a pastor anymore as it was no longer needed as Pastor Jonathan had come to visit.

Later that morning, Sharné handed me a list (in my mom's handwriting). I can recall some of the items on the list (three lemons, keys and two specific health books). I can't remember the other items but Sharné had no idea where she had gotten the list from, nor why she had even given it to me.

She said I should take my mom to lunch at *The Farmers Daughter* in Howick.

I called my mom straight away and asked her if I could take her to *The Farmers Daughter* for lunch and she said she didn't want to go. My mom knew something was terribly wrong with us – she said at the time she thought Clint had started gambling or that he may have acquired a huge debt. Terrible things were going through her own mind at the time. The devil was planting seeds of doubt. Months later, she also told us she felt her own spirit was involved and strange things were happening in her own home at the time. She said it felt as if her telephone had been tapped, that some men had come into her house, fiddled with her phone and then sped off in a vehicle. She never ever got a telephone bill after that – very strange.

All I know is that I was just desperate to have her commit her life to God because Clint and Sharné had both confirmed that my mom wasn't really serious on her first commitment, so hence my fear intensified.

I remember clearly thinking I had to collect all these items on the list that Sharné had given me. It suddenly seemed like a competition and I had to place the items in the bag and go to my mom's house as fast as possible to win the prize which was to save the planet from destruction. You must think, "Shame, this woman has lost her mind!". I was certainly in a confused state but I know today that the enemy (the devil) who is the father of all lies was having a field day in my mind.

I have no idea how many demons I had invited into my life over the years, but they were all clearly fighting for my soul.

Ntombi was there at the time and I rushed into the lounge, emptying my handbag, leaving the mess on the lounge carpet. I frantically put a bunch of keys and three lemons into my bag. I then rushed through the door and drove to *The Farmer's Daughter* in Howick.

On arrival at the restaurant, I was so confused about which specific parking lot I had to park in. I kept changing parking bays. I was petrified that I wasn't getting it right and didn't know if I should go into the restaurant. I locked my car, sat on a chair on the restaurant's verandah and cried, thinking that I had failed God on the mission I thought I was on. I was being totally derailed as I had no idea what I was doing, realising that I didn't actually know why I was even there as my mom had told me she didn't want to go there. It was a terrifying feeling, being unable to save the world from destruction, being totally out of control and that at any time it could be destroyed.

I was so anxious and still had no idea if I should go into the restaurant or not. I clearly recall looking at an old lady who was sitting with a younger lady. They were seated at a table near the front door. I stared at them for quite some time but I didn't enter and just drove home with a heavy heart and tears streaming down my face. I was, however, assured that the next day I would be able to try again and that I would be given a second chance.

That day, it felt as if the radio was commentating on my

every move. It felt as though people were tuning in to hear how I was doing and they were commenting as well. I had to switch it off as it was too distracting, keeping me from my mission and end goal. It was as if I was in a movie and the whole world was watching me. The voices in my mind were instructing me not to put on the TV, nor read any newspaper and avoid social media as that would give me too many clues on how I was faring in the challenge. I just knew I had to save the planet and at every turn I was stumbling, which made me extremely upset and anxious.

At that stage, my own phone was doing strange things. It would just lock and I would not be able to get back into it as it would not accept my code. I showed Clint who also witnessed strange things happening on it. One day, several 8's started appearing on the screen, rows and rows of them. What it meant I had no idea, but Clint and our girls witnessed it. It would not stop until Clint switched it off. My background screen would often just turn black on all the apps. These changes to my phone would happen on their own.

If I fell asleep for a little while, I would always be awakened at 3 am. I would look at my alarm clock next to my bed and think that my mom or someone had died. That morning, I sat up in bed, took out a notebook and started writing that Judaism, Islam and Christianity all worship the same God and it's all the same religion. This is complete heresy and a new age spirit was trying to confuse and deceive me.

> **Acts 4:12**
> *Nor is there salvation in any other, for there is no other name under heaven given among men by which we must be saved.*

Clint immediately knew this wasn't a correct doctrine and started correcting me instantly by saying they are not the same God and that Jesus is the only way. He knew the truth as he was brought up in a Christian home. Clint had given his life to the Lord and had been baptised as a young teenager. That solid foundation put him in good stead in knowing the truth and leading me in finding the way. Clint made sure I highlighted the verse *John 3:16* in the Bible. He wanted me to read that verse over and over again. Clint had not been a practising Christian but God did own him even though the enemy had invaded him and taken up residency in his temple – a squatter – who also knew his time was coming to an end.

I tried to gather notes on how to pray correctly, what needed to be done if someone dies and I strongly felt that God was telling me to 'come as you are'. I felt that I no longer needed to worry about makeup or doing my hair. I literally thought I must be naked. I would later recall the lyrics of Crowder's song, *Come as you are*, and smile, thinking about how I had interpreted God saying "come as you are". God says "Come as you are". He doesn't ask us to come after we have cleaned up our act. He takes us just as we are, carrying all our baggage and burdens and all our sins. If we are honest with ourselves and with God, He starts the cleansing process on the inside. He transforms us and heals our hearts. God doesn't always change our situation, but He uses the situation to change us. He won't keep us from being thrown into a fiery furnace or facing trials, but He will ensure that He will always be with us through those trials. When we come to Him just as we are, He gives us a brand-new start and hope for the future. The lies the enemy was telling me were distorting my reality and he wanted to bring shame to me by making me believe I no longer required clothes. Both my girls had to often step in to convince me to put my clothes back on. They could not believe their mother was behaving so bizarrely.

That day, all I wanted to do was wash the linen and I believed I needed to follow specific procedures in order to get it right for God. I thought He was watching me and so was the world. I don't know how many wash loads we did that day – too many to count. I was trying to write down the 10 commandments, believing that was why we were picking up all the ten-cent pieces. We needed to follow those commandments.

Clint also brought up the seven deadly sins which we tried to remember and write down. Clint mainly wanted to talk about Jesus and continued to make the girls and myself read *John 3:16* in the Bible Phil had given us. He didn't want to talk about anything else. The more I spoke about all the gods being the same God the more he pushed the narrative that Jesus is God which is the absolute truth and what the Bible teaches us when Jesus made these claims in several scriptures.

Clint demonstrated to me the different levels of heaven and told me that Jesus was sitting on the right-hand side of God the Father. He was very worried that I was not understanding the situation and became very frustrated and angry, saying I was a disobedient child of God. He would also shout at the girls to be quiet and listen as he wanted them to understand about Jesus too. This would stress me as I did not want to disappoint God. Clearly the devil was trying to confuse me with a spirit of religion. Strangely, Clint, Kelsey and I were unable to complete the *Lord's Prayer*. We attempted to pray it together but, no matter how hard we tried, none of us remembered it fully. We kept getting stuck, unable to recite all the words, yet that is a prayer we have all been taught in school, having had to recite it so many times. However, during these few days we just couldn't get it right.

That night, I felt as though I had been impregnated supernaturally. I was convinced I was pregnant and told Clint. He wondered who the dad was because he had undergone a vasectomy a few years prior so he knew it wasn't him. I asked him if we could get a pregnancy test the next day. You can imagine the worry and anguish Clint felt, knowing that it wasn't possible for him to conceive a child but, as God is our witness, in our entire marriage neither of us have ever committed adultery.

21 November 2018 – Wednesday

Clint left that morning. I have no idea where he went every day and to this day, he has no recollection where he went either but we know he wasn't going to his office in Durban and he wasn't at home. He stood at the door and kept telling me that there was one job he needed me to do for him and that was to buy a Jesus fridge magnet. He said I should try the *One Life Church Bookshop* at the South Site. He was adamant that I needed to obey him and fulfill this important task. I needed to listen to him and follow his simple instruction. I couldn't even complete this simple task, the demons clearly not wanting me to.

I called Ethan, Angela's husband, to ask him what was going on with me. I said I surely shouldn't feel like this and that I knew something was terribly wrong with me. I told him I was gripped by fear and explained how I was so scared about my mom and others dying. I told him that Clint and I hadn't slept properly for days and I was unable to eat or function properly.

He told me the devil was attacking me because God is going to use me in His Kingdom. I asked him what I should do and he told me to take olive oil and put crosses on every window in our home, anointing in the Name of the Father, the Son and the Holy Spirit. I followed his instruction and put crosses on every window – still suspecting I was being watched all the time.

By the time I arrived at the Christian bookshop, I had clean forgotten about the Jesus magnet and I was convinced I was there to buy the two books on my mom's list so I could complete the task, bring everything to her house and save the planet. The church was having a function in the hall that day. As they were busy setting up, I remember seeing a gift bag on a chair. I had a peek inside and thought, 'Oh wow! I will be presented with this gift!' I believed the function was going to be a celebration that I had completed the mission and the whole world was now safe.

I hurried into the bookshop and was devastated when the lady told me they didn't have the books I was looking for. She could clearly see I was upset and stressed and offered to call around. I must have looked like a wreck as I was convinced the Lord had told me, "Come as you are". Looking back now, I know what 'Come as you are' means – come with all your sins and burdens, confess them and Jesus will forgive you and wash you as white as snow.

The lady in the bookshop called *Bargain Books* at the mall and wrote down the names of the books and their prices. As I left One Life Church, I felt crushed and felt that everyone there was looking at me with anger and hatred in their hearts as I had failed them and the test once again and I couldn't save the earth. I drove away only to find the gate locked. I tried to call but my phone was locked. I cried frantically, feeling hopeless, not knowing what to do next. I turned the car around and realised there was another exit. I knew I needed to get to the mall.

On my way to the mall, I was stuck behind a construction vehicle with a big sign on it that read 'DANGER'. I thought, 'Oh, ok, I need to follow this truck', which I did, landing up on some hilltop at Meadow Feeds in Willowton Road. The man stopped his truck. I also stopped and he approached my car, asking me if everything was okay and if I needed help. I couldn't answer him. I just cried. I had no idea what was going on. I was derailed yet again. I sat in my car there for some time before recollecting my thoughts that I needed to get to the bookshop.

I eventually arrived at the mall and walked up and down there so many times trying to find the bookshop. I was stressed but eventually found the shop and purchased the two books which cost me R485.00. They were *Eating for Sustained Energy* (volumes 1 and 4). I thought the ladies in the bookshop were so angry with me because I had let everyone down. They seemed to be looking at me with such hatred in their eyes. It was as though everyone around was looking down at me with scolding eyes. I went to the exit boom gate and it wouldn't let me through as I had forgotten to pay for parking. I frantically reversed all the way back to the entrance. I can honestly say that I would never be able to drive like that in my own ability. I wish I could go back and watch it on camera footage. Truly, I am not a *Formula 1* race car driver but that day I certainly drove like one.

I left the mall and headed to Howick to visit my mom. Clint had spent a lot of time that morning talking to her on the phone, telling her to love me and give me a hug when she saw me. She thought he had gone mad. I told my mom something terrible was happening to me and that I couldn't eat because of all the sores in my mouth and I hadn't slept properly in days. She told me to lie down on her bed and try to sleep and she made me some chicken soup. I called my brother from my mom's house, still scared about what was happening to me. He tried to console me. I was able to eat the chicken soup which tasted delicious and my mom gave me some asparagus. I remember her putting the fork, holding the asparagus, in front of my eyes as I sat at her dining room table. She told me it was through the eye of the needle. This triggered a thought that would often creep up over the next few days. Clint and I both squinted our eyes on different and separate occasions, saying, "It's through the eye of the needle". We both had no idea that there is a scripture in the Bible which talks about the eye of the needle.

> **Matthew 19:24**
> *And again I say to you, it is easier for a camel to go through the eye of a needle than for a rich man to enter the kingdom of God.*

I gave my mom the books I had bought. She was totally puzzled and could not understand why I had bought them because she already owned both those books.

Clint arrived at my mom's house looking totally rattled. He was very restless. He told me months later he had felt that way because, when he arrived at my mom's house, I was lying in her arms – something he hadn't witnessed before so it was unfamiliar to him. He said he had a strong feeling that my mom was the wolf in sheep's clothing. But I just felt safe in my mother's arms. The enemy was also planting seeds of doubt in Clint's mind, later giving heed to a deceptive spirit, when he believed all the lies the enemy was telling him. The battle is in the mind and that is where the attack from the deceptive spirits starts. I was so confused and truthfully felt a bit scared of Clint at that stage. I began to think he was poisoning me. I lay in my mom's arms as she questioned him about all kinds of things – about fish, lunch, with whom he'd had lunch with and why he had changed our gardener's working days.

She asked him to make me a cup of tea, giving him strict instructions on where to find the tea and how to make it. Poor Clint was being interrogated and he was so overwhelmed, not feeling himself and paranoid about everything. He came back with the wrong tea and my mom shouted at him for not listening. She was planting seeds in my mind that Clint was having an affair just by her line of questioning and her actions.

I had also found a pearl earring in my mom's bed earlier and questioned her on whose it was. She said she had no idea. It's hard to explain all this but the spirit world is real and they can also plant things in the natural world to manipulate a situation and not just in our minds, of which we had experienced firsthand accounts. There was a lot of tension in the room that day. My poor mom was also very worried about us and she told Clint to go and see his mom. She said it was an instruction and not a suggestion.

Looking back, I can see how the devil works at setting traps for us to fall into because, a few weeks prior, I had received a phone call from a friend who said her husband had told her that Clint and his secretary had spent so much time together at a recent work conference, they were practically joined at the hip. She also asked me if I knew what they called the secretary at work. Of course, I said I didn't know. She said they call her 'Mrs Mey'. It was a bit like a dagger had pierced my heart, yet I remained calm and just laughed. I think the enemy was laughing much louder as, after the phone call, I contacted Clint's mom and told her the story. I was crying and felt a pang of betrayal. As I relayed the story to her, I remembered that, a year prior, Clint had said we were not going to buy Christmas presents for each other but he was only going to buy a gift for his secretary. Can you see how the enemy was hard at play creating a perfect storm?

Immediately after that phone call, I sent Clint a message asking him to meet me at the *Golden Horse Casino*, something I had never done in all our years of marriage. I just didn't want to talk to him about the situation with the kids around. He thought it was very strange but agreed to meet me there. I stepped into his car and confronted him head-on about his relationship with his secretary. He assured me there was nothing going on between them. He loved her as a friend. She was good to him and he reminded me of how kind she had been to our whole family. I believed him without a doubt and put the incident behind me. A few days later, I was at another friend's house relaying the story to her. We both cried that afternoon as she was struggling with certain issues and had confided in me. The devil was working on his schemes and strategies as he knew I was reading the Word of God. I was starting to listen to Christian music and I was drawing closer to the Lord, but the devil was planting seeds in others that there was something else going on. That is why some people didn't believe us when we told them what had happened to us. They thought it was a marriage problem, nervous breakdown, stress, menopause and that perhaps we had taken drugs.

We left my car in my mom's garage as we were flying to London the next week on holiday with Kelsey who, at this stage, had said she was not going with us to London. Shame, the poor child woke up every morning asking if the nightmare she was living was over. We would say it was and then it would just get worse.

This was having a terrible effect on both our girls. As we

drove off, there was a pack of seeds in Clint's car and we said we needed to plant seeds about the Lord. On the way home, Clint and I had an argument about my mom. Clint said she was not saved and that I should not stop drinking because she had deceived me. However, I didn't want to drink anymore anyway and the urge had totally disappeared.

I told Kelsey I was pregnant and wanted to buy pregnancy test kits. I didn't just want one, I wanted Clint to buy them all. After some arguing, he eventually agreed to buy two tests. On the way home, I heard the siren of the ambulance and I was frantic. I needed to do the test in the car. I was desperate to do the test right there and then. Poor Clint and Kelsey couldn't understand what was happening and Kelsey, who has always wanted a baby sibling, was probably so confused about what was going on. In addition to that, both girls were busy trying to study and write their year-end exams at the time. I did the tests when we arrived home and they were both negative. I still felt as if I was going to have a baby and 10 000 people would come to our home, including angels. I believed that anyone who was on the dark side would not be able to enter through our gates. I had a strong feeling that God was going to protect us from any ungodly people. I am sure this was planted from the song, *The Sound of Silence*, which I had listened to, where the lyrics read: *"10 000 people maybe more".*

I also told the girls they were going to be archangels one day. I had seen a vision of angels and the most incredible display of lights looking out into the universe, so I convinced myself that Kelsey was going to be the archangel of babies and Sharné would be the archangel of animals. It's no wonder Kelsey left home the following day. I had told Clint that his girls were going to be archangels and he believed it.

I was up in the early hours of the morning reading Clint's dad's King James Version Bible in the lounge. Amazingly enough, in the dim light with no glasses, I could read perfectly. I had been reading for quite some time when all of a sudden, the words on the pages became negative about Jesus. It scared me. I closed the Bible and put it down. I then picked it up again to read and see if I was imagining things. I continued to read and still the words were shocking about Jesus which disturbed me completely and I closed the Bible again. I immediately arose, went to the ledge at our front door, picked up the wooden buddha idol I had bought in Bali, threw it in the bin and headed to bed. That was the working of the Holy Spirit.

Exodus 20:4
You shall not make for yourself a carved image—any likeness of anything that is in heaven above, or that is in the earth beneath, or that is in the water under the earth;

I lay in bed fearing that the girls had both died. I woke Clint up, begging him to check on them to see if they were still breathing. Clint came back and said they were both fine and asleep. Living in constant fear that your mom and children and even friends are dying, or dead, is terrifying. The spirit of fear had a grip on me.

It had been over a week since they had cut a huge hole in our ceiling to replace the geyser and the company had still not returned to fix it. We had a black plastic covering over the hole. During the early hours of that morning, the black covering was making a huge noise. It was vigorously moving up and down. It seemed as though something desperately wanted to get out, as if something was trapped in our house. Clint got up again and taped the entire black plastic to the ceiling with thick sellotape but there was still something causing movement. Clint eventually decided to just tear the entire covering down and the noise stopped, bringing instant peace. It was not normal, very supernatural; it was demonic and we both knew it. Only when I reread my story to edit did it hit me like a sledge hammer… The idol I had thrown away earlier wanted to get out – the spirit that was attached to it – that is why we are told to burn them. I should have burnt it. But I have repented and God is forgiving.

> **Deuteronomy 7:25**
> *You shall burn the carved images of their gods with fire; you shall not covet the silver or gold that is on them, nor take it for yourselves, lest you be snared by it; for it is an abomination to the LORD your God.*

22 November 2018 – Thursday

When Clint got out of bed, the first thing he wanted to know was what had happened to the idol that had been on the mantlepiece. I told him I had thrown it away. He then told me that, the previous night just before going to bed, he had the biggest urge to throw it away but was worried how I would react. Instead, he just turned the idol around to face the wall. He told me he couldn't bear to look at it. He did not like that idol at all. It was amazing how the two were becoming one.

It was Kelsey's final cooking practical that morning and it was also load shedding, so the traffic was hectic. After dropping her off at school, I became frantic and I just wanted to jump out of the car – I had no idea why – I just felt extremely anxious. Clint calmed me down and drove us to the Hayfields Wimpy as I hadn't been eating properly, other than my mom's chicken soup and asparagus the day before. I would just gag. Even at night it would feel like something was trying to choke me and I would constantly have a sick feeling in the pit of my stomach. I would often ask Clint to pray for me and even Kelsey prayed for me. Clint told me that it was a fight for my soul and he had told me that most of our family and friends were on the dark side and were not walking with the Lord. Clint had identified spiritual players in the spiritual realm who he said were fighting for my soul.

He said his dad was number one in satan's kingdom, followed by Hazel, my friend for nearly 30 years, since I'd met Clint. He told me he felt that he was not on earth and the one time at the shopping mall he could identify the spirit of the person. They had a different colour shade – either a light or darkish haze – above them. The ones with the light haze would smile and look happy and the ones with the darkish haze would look angry. He had told me not to contact or speak to anyone, which I couldn't as my phone was now missing altogether after it had changed my profile picture back to my gran and grandad on its own. Clint asked me who had changed my profile picture and I recall saying it was my guardian angel. It certainly wasn't me, as my phone at this point was now missing. Only when Kelsey broke open the cupboard in our study the following week did we find my phone in there. It had been locked away and the keys were nowhere to be found. That's why she broke the door open.

We sat in the Wimpy and I was extremely paranoid. It felt like there were evil forces trying to distract me from the truth of God. We were so confused as to where to sit that we moved a few times. We sat outside then moved back in and then again went outside but eventually settled down inside. Clint ordered two breakfasts that morning and I could not eat. I was gagging the whole time and trying to block my ear from hearing a man talking about the Bible to someone on his phone in Afrikaans. I told Clint that man was there to derail me.

Clint said I had to eat. He was very concerned about me not eating. He often said 'the elf must keep nourished' but only when he took the tomato sauce and said it was the Blood of Jesus was I able to eat. He kept pouring the tomato sauce over my food, saying it was the Blood of Jesus so I could continue eating. It sounds crazy I know but it's the truth.

Leaving the Wimpy, we drove to the Christian bookshop at the *One Life Church* – South Site to look for the magnet Clint was desperate to buy. On the way there he pulled the car over and called Hazel. He said he had taken out his dad and now needed to take out Hazel who had become spiritual enemy number one in satan's kingdom. He was frantic to call her. He spoke about Roger Federer and Rafa Nadal. He spoke about them being soulmates. I can't remember the exact conversation, but I know he felt threatened by her and kept saying how powerful she was – not physically but spiritually. He had also been sending WhatsApp voice notes to his mom and dad telling them to leave me and the girls alone and to not make contact with my mom and if they did not obey him they would be taken out (we still have those voice notes on our phones as evidence) When we relistened to them it certainly was very disturbing, bizarre behavior.

There were no magnets at the bookshop, so we both sat down at a little round table in the foyer of the church feeling deflated. We both said we had been derailed. Clint became paranoid about the fridge magnet that we had to get. We drove around for approximately two hours trying to find a magnet. Clint eventually phoned a Christian work colleague, Cheryl, to ask her where we should go to buy it.

Eventually we found a Christian shop in town and Cheryl had told Clint it would be fine to buy it there. Inside the little Christian bookshop, we found the perfect magnet which read 'TRUST JESUS'. However, before we could buy it, Clint had to call Cheryl again for confirmation that this was indeed a good magnet to buy. We walked out the shop pleased with ourselves that we had completed this task and headed home with the magnet in hand.

When we arrived home, Kelsey was packing her things. She was crying and said she could no longer stay with us. She wanted her parents back. She was scared and had no idea what was going on. All she knew was that things were not normal in our home. Her friend, Brené, had invited her to stay with them.

That night there was load shedding (power outage) and Sharné had her final exam the next day. She asked if we would take her to Ashburton to her friend Stan's house so she could study there. We took her there and, on the way home, we noticed that all the electricity was on in our area. Our block was on and it felt like God's Hand was in it. When we arrived home, Clint said he was God and that God had given him power for a few minutes so I had to ask him questions. I could ask him anything and he would turn the lights on and off. We were sitting in the dining room and Clint really did put the lights on and off, using his mind and on demand. I was amazed.

Clint had always been extremely fascinated with magic and illusion and I believe he thought he was a magician. He took the magnet off the fridge, we both had to sit on the carpet in the lounge with our hands on the magnet and we had to ask God questions. I could not think of one single question. Clint kept telling me I was a disobedient child of God and became angry with me while he tried to explain how God's kingdom worked. He wanted me to get it right – that Jesus is God. I remember he was upset with me because I was not on the same level as him in the heavenlies. It scared him, and he said he didn't want us on different levels – he wanted me to be with him. I was getting worked up as I felt I did not know how to pray properly and I wasn't getting it right. Again, those are the enemy's lies as Jesus hears all our prayers and petitions. There is no formula. We just need to speak and pray to Him directly.

We had so much food in our fridge probably because Kelsey had been practising her recipes for her final practical exam and because we were not eating the food. It was rotting and the fridge was stinking. Both Clint's and my senses were very heightened. We threw out all the food and, at 10:30 pm, we headed back to fetch Sharné in Ashburton. Clint still did not have his glasses. He could not find them anywhere and he thought, for some reason, that my mom had taken them and my phone was missing. I recall telling Clint that I didn't like him anymore. He acted as if he was going to drive us into a truck that was halfway in the road. It was raining and we were totally lost. I was becoming frantic and paranoid about wanting to find Sharné. We were both screaming at each other and he said he needed to fall back in love with me.

Eventually, we found Stan's house and picked up Sharné. That night, Clint identified his dad as satan. We had driven to his parents' house earlier during the day but we didn't enter their property because the garage door just closed automatically while we were sitting in the driveway. Clint thus said we couldn't go there that day as it wasn't the right time and we drove home. He went into the study and whilst clasping his two index fingers and thumbs together, he was looking through 'the eye of the needle' and he then identified a photograph of his father and said "satan I have found you".

It was really difficult for Clint and myself to lie close to each other. One of us would be on fire and the other would be ice-cold and vice versa (just like the yin and yang chair we had seen at the braai). We smelt the most repulsive, pungent odours from each other. I already mentioned that our senses were so heightened and Clint would often pray over us. He knew we were in a spiritual battle in another realm.

It felt as though witchcraft spells had been cast on us and Clint would mention different spells to me – spells cast on us in our past. Only two years later did we find out that one of those spells cast on Clint and his brother had been performed by a family member who used a doll with pins to curse them and practised witchcraft spells over them.

Something was wanting to keep us apart – something very dark and evil. We weren't imagining this it really happened to us. Months later in April 2019, whilst visiting Clint's family in Cape Town, we told them what had happened to us. Clint's cousin then told us there was a line of white witches in his family and his grandmother had once been a tarot card reader. Apparently, a generational curse had been placed on all marriages in the family and ours was the last standing marriage of all the grandchildren in the family line. We may never know if that played a part in our spiritual warfare or not, but the truth of the matter is that the unseen world is real and only God can open our eyes to see it. There is a fight happening around us every day, a battle raging for our souls and the Bible is very clear about this. I think deep down we all know this. God's Spirit is in every born-again believer and that's why so many people won't go to fortune-tellers, soothsayers, witchdoctors or play ouija board and glassy glassy – because we know it is wrong and it's really dangerous.

Exodus 34:7
Keeping mercy for thousands, forgiving iniquity and transgression and sin, by no means clearing the guilty, visiting the iniquity of the fathers upon the children and the children's children to the third and the fourth generation.

In the early hours of the morning, looking at the alarm clock next to my bed, it read 3 am. I heard Lexi, our blind Labrador, crying and howling. I told Clint that she was dying and I needed to go and see her. Clint told me I was being ridiculous, but I insisted on going outside to see her. I was getting myself worked up thinking she was dying.

Clint came outside with me and I just sat there, hugging Lexi. Her head kept lifting my chin up as I sat there hugging her. She kept pushing my head up, making me look up to the sky. It felt as though she was saying, "Look up! look up to Jesus!" Clint, on the other hand, just sat there hugging his two boys, Charlie and Luca, our golden retrievers. When we went back inside, I told Clint he had broken my heart. He was confused and couldn't understand why. I told him it was because I had said Lexi was dying and he didn't even touch her. He only paid attention to Charlie and Luca. He went into the shower and started crying. When he came out, I took the cream which the lady had given me the previous weekend called Nourish and rubbed him down from head to toe. I asked him when he had given his life to the Lord and he said when he was a teenager. I told him he had to recommit and give his life to the Lord again. I felt like I was anointing his body.

In the early hours of the morning, Clint said the Lord had given him a clear vision in a dream. He said that the dogs represented his family – Luca was Sharné, Charlie was Kelsey and our black blind Labrador, Lexi, was me. He said

God showed him that the order in our house was wrong. He said that I was at the bottom of his priorities and that the kids were at the top. He said God showed him the way he treated our blind lab was the way he was treating me and that he needed to restore order in his house – biblical order. God showed Clint how he took his two golden retrievers for a daily walk but that he always left the blind Labrador behind and she would cry and howl as they left without her; that because she was blind, he would feed her a little less of the treats and he certainly paid her no attention. Clint said from that moment he knew he had to restore order in our home. We lay there until the sun came up, confessing all our sins to each other, opening up to each other about our deepest darkest secrets.

> **James 5:16**
> *Confess your trespasses to one another, and pray for one another, that you may be healed. The effective, fervent prayer of a righteous man avails much.*

That morning, Clint told me I was more precious to him than rubies – words that were also written on the Nourish cream I had rubbed him down with earlier.

> **Proverbs 31:10**
> *Who can find a virtuous wife? For her worth is far above rubies.*

23 November 2018 – Friday

Lack of sleep was certainly taking its toll on me, together with still not being able to eat properly. When Clint came back from his early morning run, Luca broke loose and started running wildly in the road. He screamed for Sharné to 'go fetch herself'. The previous night, God had shown him in a dream that she was Luca and he was taking it literally. The fact that I had told him she was going to be the archangel of animals made it even worse as now he thought she needed to work on her animal skills and get her dog under control. The neighbours were outside, hearing all the commotion and Clint told them not to stress because God was restoring order in our home.

Sharné was crying as she was being scolded at to control her dog. A lady was walking her own dog and was shouting at Sharné for the same thing. She threatened to taser Luca. I have mentioned before that our dogs were extremely wild during this time as if they were possessed themselves. They were unruly and disobedient and wouldn't listen to anybody. My neighbour was still standing next to the wall and I looked at her in total horror and disbelief that she found the situation amusing. I was terrified at what was going on around me and felt I couldn't even talk to her as I was being watched and under surveillance.

Managing at last to get Luca back into the yard, Sharné was now ready to write her final exam that morning and I frantically begged her not to go. I told her there would be no-one writing the exam. I was convinced it was the end of the world as I had failed all my tests and I could no longer save the planet. I was wailing, petrified, not wanting her to leave. The more I begged her, the angrier she became. The poor child was sobbing, telling me she would call the police if I did not let her go to write the exam. She said she was not going to rewrite this exam next year. I was holding onto her, not wanting to let go. She thought I had gone completely mad and pushed past me, stepped into her car and drove off to write her final exam. I thank God for giving her the courage and wisdom to get through that exam and all the others too for that matter. I now know that it was only by God's grace that she passed all her exams with distinctions as it could not have been an easy time for her, seeing her parents as we were and not understanding what was happening to both of us.

I spoke to my mom that morning and told her once again that something was terribly wrong. She said she had made a call to our family doctor and had spoken to the receptionist. She told me to see the doctor as soon as possible. I agreed as I felt as if I was being poisoned and I wanted every drug test done. I had no means of transport, so I had to wait for Sharné to come home after writing her exam. The minute she walked through the doorway, I asked her to drive me to the doctor's rooms and I landed up seeing the doctor on duty – not my usual doctor. Whilst in the waiting room, I recall the receptionist getting up to open the door for a cat and showing me what looked like insurance documents. I just ignored her and really didn't understand what she was doing. She stood there, not saying a word, waving these papers in front of me. My mind was telling me that I needed protection and insurance cover on my life.

I didn't mention this to Clint at all and, a few days later, he told me someone had taken out an insurance policy on my life and I needed to find out who it was. Of course, no-one had but, at the time, he really believed it was true and at that stage it made me think of the receptionist who had tried to make me aware of a policy. Sharné came into the doctor's rooms with me. I wasn't able to sit still and I kept standing up and walking to the door. I was paranoid, not knowing who I could trust. It felt as though it was all a big conspiracy and I was being poisoned by someone. Truthfully, that day I thought it was Clint and our domestic helper, Ntombi, who were poisoning me.

I told the doctor I couldn't sleep and I hadn't eaten properly for days because of all the sores in my mouth. They were so painful which made eating and drinking all the more difficult. I told the doctor I was also unable to function in my own home. The minute I walked into my house, it was as if something took over me and I would literally walk around in circles, unable to get anything done. I was up and down like a yoyo in the doctor's rooms that day and paranoia kicked in of note. I was unclear if I should even have been there. I told him someone may have been poisoning me and I wanted him to do every drug test possible to verify this.

I have no idea what he thought at the time as he sat there, not knowing what advice to give me. We left his rooms and I paid for the consultation before heading next door to have the blood tests done. I paid the bill at 1:12 pm. The reason I say this is because the demonic spirit world can plant things in your cars, houses, anywhere actually, as you will later see, that can blur your judgement and distort reality for the sake of getting their plans and schemes into the forefront of your mind where the battle rages.

We were the only people in the blood testing clinic and, as I sat down, Clint called to ask me where I was. I told him I was at the doctor's rooms having every test done so I could see what I was being poisoned with. He was very irritated and told me to wait before I did anything and hung up. He was truly worried, believing my soul was in danger.

We sat with the nurse and listened to her tell us all about her son. She showed us a poem he had written which hung on the wall in her office. Sharné and I were both touched and moved by the poem and both became a little teary-eyed. Just as I was finishing off completing all the necessary paper work for the blood tests, Clint stormed in. He fanatically demanded that the lady tell him whether or not she had a Bible. She said she did and Clint asked her for it. He made me read *John 3:16*, after which he threw himself on the floor and started shouting for God to take him. He said he had made a 3-for-2 deal, bearing in mind it was *Black Friday* that day, and that the Lord must take him and leave us. He was screaming so loudly that the entire rooms must have heard him. The doctor I had seen heard all the commotion and came outside to meet us as we were leaving. He handed me an envelope addressed to a doctor at Akeso Clinic, saying I should go there.

Sharné was extremely shaken up and full of tears yet again. She left in her own car as Clint had said I would go home with him. Getting into Clint's car, I begged him to take me to the place that was mentioned on the envelope. I had never heard of the place before nor did I have any idea where it was. Clint refused. He put his car seat back and started begging God to take him again, carrying on about how I needed to give my life to save his because he had given his life to save his three girls. I kept on saying I would only give my life to save the planet. Clint and I eventually arrived home. He was on his phone all the time. He told me he had figured out what was going on and he was making *Black Friday* deals. Clint was making deals with one of his colleagues at work who asked if he was still going to London. Clint told him that he wasn't going anymore as he was going to house-sit but that I was going and he could have our accommodation but not the air tickets, a 3-for-2 deal. Then he told him he could have the tickets and not accommodation. We only looked at all the messages on Clint's phone a few weeks later, realising this was totally unusual behaviour, both from messages made and from ones received. I, on the other hand, had no cellphone so I was unable to communicate with anyone.

When we arrived back home, I found a King Shaka Airport parking ticket in Clint's car and wondered why he had been there. I wondered whom he was seeing and meeting up with as there was no reason for him to have been there. My mind was racing. I recalled him pulling out the suitcases earlier that morning and the thought had crossed my mind that he was leaving me or flying somewhere with someone else. I hadn't realised that Clint was retrieving all the suitcases as Sharné was leaving for Australia on Sunday and he still thought we were going to London on Tuesday.

This is what I mentioned earlier – how things can be planted by the spirit realm as the ticket I had found read that he had driven in to King Shaka Airport on the 23rd November 2018 at 12:38. This made it impossible to have been at the doctor's rooms 35-40 minutes later, a 108 km drive from the King Shaka Airport to the doctor's rooms in Town bush Road, Pietermaritzburg. Clint had been nowhere near the Durban Airport that day and we later checked his toll records to determine what had gone on. As crazy as it sounds, the spirit world is real and we realised this was planted in his car to create fear, paranoia and doubt in my mind, causing me to have further trust issues. Not only was he now poisoning me but he was planning on leaving me too. The enemy wanted to destroy me and my family.

The repair team also arrived that morning to fix our ceiling. They replaced the entire passage ceiling and by that afternoon they had completed the job. I asked the workers if they were Christians and they said they were. I told them how thankful we were for all their hard work and that we needed to pray over our house. Clint and I, together with Ntombi and all the workers stood in the passage, holding hands and lifting our prayers to the Lord.

Late Friday afternoon after the workers had packed up, we headed to Clint's parents' house. His parents later admitted they were petrified of us at the time, unsure as to what we were capable of, as they had never seen us like this before. The threatening voice notes Clint and I were sending to them had sent shivers down their spine. Clint's mom then contacted Phil and Charmaine requesting them to join us as they were extremely nervous to be alone with us. They in turn had asked two elders from One Life South Church to join us at Clint's parents' home. Clint's mom was convinced I had done something to her son. I clearly remember feeling an overwhelming threat over my life as I sat down, so much so that I took off my socks and left them under the couch as evidence that I had been there. I truly felt I was going to be poisoned and sacrificed right there in their lounge.

When Phil and Charmaine arrived, we noticed she was only wearing one pearl earring. That made me think of the pearl earring I had seen at my mom's house on Wednesday when she had planted a seed that Clint was having an affair with someone who had something to do with tea. Charmaine had given us herbal tea the previous Sunday on our visit there. My mom did not even realise what she was doing or even why she was doing certain things which she later discussed with us. Clint greeted Charmaine with a hug and he practically pushed her away, telling her she stank and that he detected the same smell on her that he was smelling on me. She was very offended and embarrassed, looking at her husband, Phil, asking him if she smelt bad. He told her she didn't. Clint's dad apologised to her for his son's behaviour but our senses were so heightened – the smell of tea and certain perfumes had become so pungent to us. At times, Clint and I smelt like dead rats to each other and we couldn't bear to be near one another.

I was paranoid and recall Clint's mom giving me a piece of meat on a bone to eat. I thought it had been laced with poison and that it was a test of my faith. For a brief moment, I trusted God and felt no fear as I ate a piece of the meat. It was the first time I had eaten meat since temporarily giving it up a few days earlier. My emotions were being torn – shredded into tiny pieces. I went from feeling intense fear to calmness and *vice versa.* It's extremely hard to put into words as I sound like I'm contradicting myself. That is the fight – good against evil – the battle for your soul. Clint's mom looked at me with wild eyes. There was a rage in her look that I had never seen before. She stared at me with such intensity. I will never forget the way she stared at me. I sensed that she blamed me for what was going on.

However, I had no idea what was going through her mind at the time. I realise now she was petrified for us and scared for her youngest son, her baby, whom she had never seen or heard behave like this before. In all his years on this earth, he was a loving, kind son who was now accusing them of being evil and on the dark side – accusing his mom of molesting him and casting spells on him as a baby. The devil had planted seeds in Clint's mind that his own mom had abused him as a child which is totally bizarre and untrue and that his dad was the devil – satan himself. We now know how the enemy works but at the time we believed all the lies he was telling Clint and me.

John 8:44
You are of your father the devil, and the desires of your father you want to do. He was a murderer from the beginning, and does not stand in the truth, because there is no truth in him. When he speaks a lie, he speaks from his own resources, for he is a liar and the father of it.

Clint and I must have looked like absolute wrecks sitting in their lounge. Clint's parents hadn't seen us for days and I had told them God had said, "Come as you are". My hair was untidy, all over the place, unbrushed and I was dressed very scruffily. I had also lost about seven kilograms, my weight reducing to 48 kg. It's no wonder that, a few months later, one of the elders who was there that afternoon didn't even recognise us at a school parents' evening. When Clint and I greeted him, he had no idea we were the ones whom he had come to pray over. He looked absolutely shocked when we told him he had come to Clint's parents' house a few months earlier. That shows how different we must have looked.

We all sat in the lounge and they asked us a few questions which we tried to answer. One elder said what we were explaining that was happening to us was certainly not Christianity. They had no idea what was going on with us and they were most likely not equipped to deal with such situations. Whether we were oppressed or possessed, I do not know, but there was a fight raging around us. Clint was becoming very agitated with his dad and he put his dad's Bible on the floor in the middle of the lounge. He became very angry and shouted at Clint to pick it up. Clint then told him, "Today is about you and me and you will be exposed when we pray the sinner's prayer" which his dad managed to do and that totally baffled Clint as he now thought his dad couldn't be satan or he would not have been able to say the sinner's prayer and confess that Jesus is Lord.

Phil sat next to Clint on the couch and had his arm around him. I recall thinking that was just strange. The way he was holding onto Clint made me feel uncomfortable. The poor chap was just concerned for his friend but my mind was telling me something else.

Clint and I were told to stand up in the middle of the lounge and the others surrounded us. They all prayed over us and I honestly thought this was a cult. Some were praying in tongues and that was new to me. I thought I was being sacrificed but I was at peace knowing where I was going if I died. Today I thank them for trying their utmost to help us. They were trying to do their best for us. Praying in tongues is biblical and a spiritual gift imparted by the Holy Spirit.

1 Corinthians 14:2
For he who speaks in a tongue does not speak to men but to God, for no one understands him; however, in the spirit he speaks mysteries.

Acts 2:4
And they were all filled with the Holy Spirit and began to speak with other tongues, as the Spirit gave them utterance.

Mark 16:17
And these signs will follow those who believe: In My name they will cast out demons; they will speak with new tongues.

As I said, I don't think any of them had dealt with this sort of scenario or situation before. The deliverance ministry is required in instances like this but God was still in control and we must never forget that. No-one read from the Bible that day, our sword which, looking back now, is our most powerful weapon to use against the enemy in spiritual warfare. Even Jesus Himself, when tempted by satan, used the Word of God against him.

Hebrews 4:12
For the word of God is living and powerful, and sharper than any two-edged sword, piercing even to the division of soul and spirit, and of joints and marrow, and is a discerner of the thoughts and intents of the heart.

A few months later, Clint's dad told us that after we had left that Friday early evening, he lay down on his bed with a heavy heart. He had been a practising and faithful Christian for many years but was in a backslidden state. He was no longer serving the Lord the way he knew he should. He said God had spoken to him clearly that evening and told him that satan was trying to steal his son and me. He said God was going to give him another chance and that he had to repent of all his sins.

1 John 1:9
If we confess our sins, He is faithful and just to forgive us our sins and to cleanse us from all unrighteousness.

He said he lay on his bed repenting of his sins and recommitted his life to Jesus that very evening. He told us God supernaturally changed him in that very moment and he was instantly delivered from his alcohol and gambling addictions as well as other strongholds.

We left Clint's folks' home, still unclear about what was happening to us, feeling very stressed and uneasy. I was constantly being tormented and truly still unable to function properly when I arrived home. Thus, we once again called Pastor Jonathan, begging him to come to our house. He was kind enough to agree and gave freely of his time.

Sharné wasn't home at the time we arrived and I was panicking about where she was. It was raining and Clint said she had gone to the Pot and Barrel Pub in Hilton. I couldn't understand how he had let her go out in her car in that weather. He was normally so protective over her. Clint told me he was giving her car to her friend, Stan, and that he had decided to give our house and my car to the Pastor. His lack of concern for Sharné's whereabouts greatly disturbed me.

Pastor Jonathan and his wife, Rebecca, arrived a short while later. Clint was totally on edge. He was up and down and very restless. I was paranoid that he was poisoning me and recall spitting into the glass of water just in case it was laced with something. The pastor didn't touch his water either. Clint rushed off to the study and brought back a photo of my grandfather, my mother and me.

He placed it in front of me and asked me in a very stern voice, "What is wrong with this picture?" I was confused at his question and he kept asking me, "Where is the wife?" He was trying to tell me my grandfather was my dad and that he had molested me as a child. Clint said he had read my diary journal of my England holiday from my childhood the previous night. He said in our 21 years of marriage, he had never ever seen this diary journal before and now suddenly it had appeared in his briefcase, so he began reading it. He told me the diary intrigued him and he wanted to know who the puppet master was in Norwich. He said my entries just ended abruptly one day when I went to granddad's house and that was when the devil had planted seeds that I had been molested as a child. At one stage, he even thought my mother and brother had done something to me.

Of course, all of it was untrue but I understand now how real it felt to him because I was having my own battles in my mind. The things Clint was telling me were crazy and bizarre but I believed every word. He told me that most people were evil and he identified them by placing them in teams – Clint's team, the good guys whom he called God's team, and Mary-Ann's team, the bad guys. Pastor Jonathan told me months later that the first time he came to visit us he sensed something was wrong with me and the second time he visited, he felt something was wrong with Clint. But truly, something was terribly wrong with both of us.

Later, Sharné arrived home along with, her friends, Rachel and Rob. I begged her not to go out, but off she went and I couldn't blame her. She told me nearly two years later that she had never cried so much as during those hectic days. To this day, both our children do not like to talk about what happened in our home. They have put it behind them.

Pastor Jonathan and his wife, Rebecca, prayed and sang with us. Just before leaving, he said something to me in the lounge that I thought was to assist me regarding being poisoned. He told me to take acid sooner rather than later, possibly referring to antacid. However, at that stage, I interpreted this to be acid which would neutralise the poison in my system. After they left, I rushed to the kitchen to find acid. I picked up a tiny purple bottle of tissue salts (No. 10) which was on the kitchen counter. I read the word 'acidity'. Relieved, I immediately thought that was what I needed to take, these tiny white tablets, to help me with all the sores on my tongue and in my mouth and that would break down or neutralise whatever I was being poisoned with.

I popped one or two of these tissue salt tablets in my mouth and continued to take one or two daily going forward. Unfortunately, that didn't do anything to help my situation which of course it wouldn't have.

Clint was continually playing the CD's he had been given and specifically repeated a song that says *'Jesus, I'll do what You say'*. I told him I wanted to sleep in Sharné's room that night but he became angry with me and said I had to stay with him. I couldn't understand why he wouldn't allow me to sleep in her room because he had been able to sleep anywhere in the house previously and no one questioned it. I was really scared of him that night. He had also lost it because he couldn't find the Bible that had been next to his bed. He said he had to have it. It was a Bible that Phil had given him and I remember it had a red cover with a white arrow on it. We eventually found the Bible in the study and Clint immediately calmed down, placing the Bible next to his bed.

During the past few days, supernatural things had happened in our home. One night, Clint said God told him to pray over me. He told me he kept stopping as he was exhausted but that God kept telling him to continue to pray. He said he prayed over me for one and a half hours, rebuking satan and it was the most exhausting thing he has ever had to do. He prayed until I suddenly woke up and started violently convulsing as though demon possessed. He said I convulsed 10 times. It was the scariest thing he had ever experienced in his life.

Clint said no-one would ever convince him that was me acting as he said it would be impossible for me to do that without suffering injury. I told Clint that I thought I was in a movie and I still remember winking in the dark at the ceiling on the last convulsion. I could only remember the last one but he said no-one can act like that. The demons in me, however, were trying to convince me otherwise, telling me I was in a movie.

Unknowingly, the Holy Spirit had led Clint into warfare prayer over me, just as the Apostle Paul tells us that *"our struggle is not against flesh and blood, but against the rulers, against the authorities, against the powers of this dark world and against the spiritual forces of evil in the heavenly realms"*. Therefore, our weapons to overcome these powers of darkness are not carnal or worldly, but they are divine and spiritual.

Warfare prayer is prayer that takes this scripture very seriously and engages the powers of darkness in the spirit realm with the spiritual weapons we are given, namely the Blood of Christ, the authority of His Name; the Sword of the Holy Spirit (the Word of God) and the power of the Holy Spirit exercised through faith. I was possessed and being controlled by demons. I even recall once, in the shower, doing a total backward contortion move. I could have really injured myself but I was told to 'think big' and do something radical for the movie I thought I was in. I would never be able to do that if you were to ask me today. The truth is that the legal rights I had given satan over my life by inviting in all these demonic spirits were now not happy with me as I was being drawn to the light – the bright light of Christ.

I know this all sounds super-crazy and I must remind you that we are a normal everyday family. However, this really did happen to us. I would have to get in and out the shower numerous times because I did not get the order of things right. There was a strict order I believed I needed to follow and if I didn't get it right, I would fail the assignment. I was drawn to using natural and organic products. I recall the one day, whilst in the shower, Sharné and Clint were shouting at me at the top of their lungs from our bathroom window, telling me to hurry up and stop wasting water. I had been showering for a long time and, in my mind, I thought, 'What are they talking about? God creates the water and He will provide more if we need it'. Deodorant cans would be moved around our home and both Clint and I said it felt like they were messages to us – *Playgirl, Playboy* and *Tropical* – everything we looked at spoke to us in a sense. Clint would look at the satin dental tape and think satan was messing around – which of course we know he was at the time.

Our mugs would have meanings – the London mug would

mean we should move there; the Switzerland mug would mean we should go there to watch the Laver Cup tennis. It was just so strange and not of this world. Absolutely everything we looked at seemed to have hidden meanings and we both felt this. One evening, a candle was lit in our kitchen. We checked with the girls as to who did this and why. No-one had an explanation! When my dad had passed away in April 2014, we lit a candle on the window sill in our kitchen in remembrance of him and now I felt the lit candle was for my mother. Tears streamed down my face as I was constantly being tortured thinking that my mom had died.

Clint said this was a serious spiritual battle for my soul and he kept praying for me. He was truly worried about me and it terrified him that I was not on the same level as he was. I have never felt so sick in all my life. The deceit of satan today is his illusive power to deceive.

Clint had committed his life to God as a child and had been baptised when he was 13-years-old, so God owned him legally even though the demons had occupied him and I truly now believe that his spirit man was leading him in scriptures and keeping him focused on Jesus. He hadn't read or owned a Bible and yet, during this period, the first scripture he received and quoted was Isaiah 60:22: *"When the time is right I, the LORD, will make it happen."* He just knew things that wouldn't be possible to know without supernatural intervention. Where had Clint ever even heard of spiritual warfare before? He hadn't and he just knew it was a battle for my soul. He said he knew he was not on earth and it was a spiritual and supernatural experience. I have read that a Christian cannot be possessed by a demon but they can be oppressed. I am, however, not too sure how it works if you are truly not born-again. It's one thing to say and profess that you are a Christian, but entirely different to be truly born-again – born of the Spirit.

John 3:3
Jesus answered and said to him, "Most assuredly, I say to you, unless one is born again, he cannot see the kingdom of God."

I do believe that Clint had been oppressed by evil spirits trying to distort the truth and trying to keep him from his true destiny and the path that God had mapped out for him. He was not living a godly life. Thus, if we look at *John 1:5-6:* *⁵ This is the message which we have heard from Him and declare to you, that God is light and in Him is no darkness at all. ⁶ If we say that we have fellowship with Him, and walk in darkness, we lie and do not practice the truth",* it shows us how we can be deceived by all the demonic activities that we allowed into our lives over the years. This allowed the devil access by giving him legal rights for evil spirits to invade our bodies.

The Apostle Paul makes a strong case for the possibility of Christians unwittingly opening themselves up to demonic involvement and possible entrapment and infestation through their worldly associations. The Apostle Paul also warns Christians not to participate in any pagan things. Activities, such as participating in yoga and attending a 'fun' Halloween party, are dangerous. Again, when looking back at all the things we were getting up to which were totally contradictory to the Bible and how to live a Christian lifestyle, it definitely speaks to the fact that satan and his demons had invaded both Clint and I with his lies and deceit.

I, on the other hand, certainly felt as if I were possessed and the enemy tried by all means to silence me. Many people will turn round and say, 'Christians are so judgmental and they think that they are holier than thou', but the truth is the Bible is so clear on how we can all be so easily deceived. The devil does not want to make our walk with Jesus easy and he will try by all means necessary to silence us, blind us, sear our conscience and not speak about Jesus and the salvation that is offered for all mankind. As Christians we are certainly not to judge non-believers, but are to hold our brothers and sisters in Christ accountable as the Bible teaches.

So much had happened during the past week. I recall trying to have some rest and Clint told me to lie down the one day. As I did, Ntombi started sweeping loudly outside my bedroom. I asked her to stop and then Petros, our gardener, began picking the pavement right outside my bedroom window. Every single time I lay down, I felt I had to get up. It was as though I was being told I couldn't sleep, that it was unacceptable to rest and that I needed to be busy for God. That was part of the enemy's strategy to keep me in this state – tired, weak and affecting my ability to even think rationally – like keeping me on a hamster wheel.

That night, Clint said we had to take communion with milk and bananas. Over the next three days, Clint became obsessed with milk and bananas. In a sense it was like mocking the Holy Communion but to Clint it was a symbol of his commitment to God. I was up again at 3 am and started reading a diet document which my friend, Debbie, had given me from our doctor. I was suddenly struck with the most terrible feeling that Debbie had died. I sat in the bathroom and sobbed for two solid hours. The devil is the father of all lies and he was having a field day with me. You would not believe how many tears I had cried over that past week.

24 November 2018 – Saturday

I woke up after nodding off for an hour or so. I had to drop off Sharné at the Hayfields Mall as she was going to have her nails done. I don't really know why she didn't just drive herself there that morning. However, I landed up taking her there myself in her car. When I dropped her off, she asked me if I was going to visit my mom and I had said I wasn't.

I drove home and when I reached the corner of Dennis Road and Laurence Crescent, something told me to visit my mom. The minute I turned into Stuart Road, I knew something had now taken over my car and I knew what was going to happen. It flashed in front of my eyes. I knew I had to trust God to protect me and it felt like another test of faith. I could feel my car picking up speed and I braked twice. I was immediately convicted and said "I am sorry, God. I do trust You and I am not a disobedient child of God." I said, "I do put all my trust in You, God." The next thing I knew, I woke up with a little girl's wide eyes looking at me through my driver's window. She was clearly in shock and I was unable to open my car door because of the impact of Sharné's car going through their gate, crashing into an old Jetta in the driveway and pushing that Jetta into their lounge. I kicked the door open of Sharné's car and said I was sorry to the young girl standing there. The airbag had not deployed either. I did not have one scratch on me – no cuts, no bruises not even whiplash, nothing! I had no injuries whatsoever. That's how God had his angels protected me that morning. Thank You, Jesus, for Your protection!

I know I was not driving my car that day. There were two girls on the property that morning. They asked me if I wanted a cup of tea. I first said 'yes' and sat down on the couch. Then I became very paranoid because both of them said I could not use their cellphones because they had no airtime and they said their home phone wasn't working either. This troubled me immensely because I needed to call Clint, so I decided to walk home. I needed to tell him about the accident. I crossed the field to go back home and

I knew God had saved me that morning. I arrived home to find Clint on the phone with my mom. I told him that I had crashed Sharné's car and it disturbed me even more that he didn't even blink an eye. It was as if he didn't even care. He told me to lie down. He didn't ask me about the car or anything about the accident. He wasn't concerned about the car as he said it was only a material possession. He showed no interest in taking me back to the accident either, so I walked back there myself.

When I was back at the scene of the accident, there were two ambulances there and I saw a man in a wheelchair who was very upset about his house. I told the ambulance staff to check me out as I had been the one driving the car. They all just stared at me with a blank expression and looked at me as if I was crazy. They did not even take my blood pressure and showed no concern whatsoever about my wellbeing. I found this behaviour absolutely absurd, that they were not checking if I was okay. I recall the man in the wheelchair now crying about his roof and all the damage I had done to his house. I told him it would all be sorted out. A gentleman approached me, handing me his towing card. He was from *Mac's Towing*. I was terribly confused about the situation.

It seemed that everyone was keeping a close eye on me, yet no-one actually wanting to communicate properly with me. I was feeling restless and uncomfortable. I crossed the road and stood by the lamppost. A car stopped and the driver looked at the accident scene. I asked the occupants of the vehicle if they would please take me to the hospital as the ambulances there were not willing to assess me. They said they could not as they were in a hurry and had no time to take me to the hospital.

While I was standing on the opposite side of the road, I was approached by a young man who required my cell number and I clearly remember writing it down for the gentleman as well as writing GOD HAS A PLAN and I walked back home. The accident was mentioned on a group chat that both Clint and I belong to, yet neither of us received those messages. When I finally found my phone, there was no talk of the accident on the group chat and only in December did Kyle tell me he had read about it on the group. I was totally shocked and surprised that we hadn't seen those messages. Kyle then took screen shots of the chat and sent them to me.

God has an amazing way of intertwining all our relationships, like a well thought out tapestry. He is so detailed in everything. Months later, we joined a connect group and the one evening they had asked us to share a brief summary of our testimony. That evening, there was a lady at the group whom I had not met before. Her name was Helen and, after telling them about the car accident and how God had protected me, she stood up to give me a hug, showing me her goosebumps.

She told us she lives just around the corner from where that accident took place. She said she recalled it very clearly as, that same morning of the accident, she and her husband were going for a cycle, something they often do together. However, that specific morning, her husband went back into the house while she waited on her bicycle. She told me he had kept her waiting for about 10 minutes for no reason at all. She was angry with him for making her wait for no apparent reason as he had no idea what he was going into the house for. When they rode around the corner, the first thing they saw was the accident. They stopped their bicycles to ask people when it had happened. When the people replied about 10 minutes prior, she said she went absolutely cold. She and her husband looked at each other in disbelief.

They knew right then that God had protected them from the accident. The anger towards her husband disintegrated in a flash and she was so thankful that Almighty Heavenly Father had protected them. Out of all the connect groups in Pietermaritzburg, on the night we share our testimony, a lady confirms how God had saved her and her husband from that exact same accident...a coincidence? I think not – that's what you call a 'God incident'.

The police arrived at our house shortly thereafter requesting Clint to go to the accident scene and to sort out the paper work at the police station.

When I went to the study that afternoon, our briefcase just flung on its own, hitting the study door and dropping to the floor. No-one touched it. It flung supernaturally with force and, when I looked down, the briefcase was open and our will had fallen out. I immediately thought that Clint had tried to kill me in the car accident and wanted me dead, which is why the Will had fallen out. It was a warning to me. I was made to believe that my husband, who loves me with all his heart, was actually capable of killing me. That was the strategy of the enemy, convincing me that it all made perfect sense.

The poisoning had not worked so now he was trying to kill me by other means. I asked him if he had sorted out all the paper work for the car accident. I was paranoid and wanted him to take me to the police station. I needed to report the accident myself and I asked him if he wanted to change our will. He said we could change it if I wanted to but he had no idea what was going on. I told him he didn't even care that I had been in an accident and that I had written off our daughter's car. I can't explain it, but it felt like a conspiracy against me. The enemy was lying to me, deceiving me and trying by all means possible to turn me against my husband through lack of trust and paranoia.

The police station was quiet, rather eerie for a Saturday afternoon but, even though we were the only people there, we were made to wait for ages. Eventually I was shown the accident report that the lady, whose car I had driven into, had written and I couldn't make any sense of it. However, the police did not require me to make another statement. They told me I would have to do a 24-hour accident report for the insurance company.

When we arrived home, Sharné cornered me. She was very worried about me and had looked up mind control. Sharné was now convinced that Clint was brainwashing me and she showed me things she had 'googled' and researched on her cellphone. She told me my car had been left at my mom's so I had no transport. I had no cellphone, thus having no contact with others. Clint had convinced me that everyone was evil. He had made me write notes which said I had to obey God and obey Clint who was a disciple of God and, if I didn't, the wrath of God would be poured out on me and I would be punished.

He was constantly playing repetitive music. She said, "Mom, he is brainwashing you". Clint was extremely paranoid, wanting to know what Sharné was telling me. He had not convinced the girls that they needed to give their lives to save his and had said he was dying that night. He had made a 1-for-3 deal and was waiting for God to take him. He was prepared to give his life for his three girls and the enemy had convinced him he was dying that very night. He knew Jesus and that was all Clint spoke about, so he was at peace waiting for the Father to fetch him.

> **John 15:13**
> *Greater love has no one than this, than to lay down one's life for his friends.*

From my bedside table drawer, I pulled out my small brown photo album, the same one I had shown Sharné, just before I found my diamond from years earlier. The very first photo was my grandfather, my grandmother and me. I displayed all the photos on the bed with that one right at the top and screamed for Clint. I asked him "What do you see?". He had no idea what I was talking about and again I asked him, "What do you see?" I then pointed to the photo right at the top and said "There is the wife!" I was excited to show him that in fact my grandfather was not my dad after all. I was at peace.

I refused point blank to sleep in our room that night. I was now totally convinced that he was doing something to me and it really scared me. I was totally confused, walking around like a zombie, unable to function. I was restless, up and down all night in Sharné's room, which drove her mad, but I could not sleep. She kept telling me to lie down and sleep. I remember feeling supernatural tears just rolling down my cheeks. It is just so difficult to put all this into words and I suppose it will be even harder for people to believe that all this even happened, but it did. All of it is true, as bizarre as it sounds.

I was so restless and got up to check on Clint. He had fallen asleep with the laptop playing Christian music. I closed the laptop and put it next to his bed. I don't know what deal he had made with whom but I had told him time and time again I was only prepared to give my life to save the planet. I clearly had a new age spirit in me along with other unclean spirits, confusing me with all the rituals I needed to do – not eating meat, saving the planet and focusing on the universe rather than focusing on the most important issue which was Jesus Christ.

Looking back now, I would give my life for Clint's as the

Bible teaches. A marriage is a very important covenant to God.

Ephesians 5:25
Husbands, love your wives, just as Christ also loved the church and gave Himself for her.

Genesis 2:24
Therefore a man shall leave his father and mother and be joined to his wife, and they shall become one flesh.

Matthew 19:6
So then, they are no longer two but one flesh. Therefore what God has joined together, let not man separate.

I thank God every day for his protection over my life. He had me covered during the accident. I know this because, years earlier when I was about 16-years-old, a friend drove his car into a small tree up Old Howick Road and I was taken to the hospital in an ambulance. I needed stitches in both my legs as well as on my left eye and my forehead. So, this time, by not even having a scratch, I knew, just like the red car incident which had happened in August, that God had protected me from the demonic force that was trying to kill me.

I learnt much later, after my mom's death, that God sometimes takes away the hedge of protection from around us so satan can enter our lives in a way not normally permitted, so that he can inflict on us the full extent of his strategies. However, we must not forget that those attacks come under the strict supervision of the Almighty and He only permits what is in accordance with His eternal plans and purpose He has for us. If you read the book of Job in the Bible, it will testify to the statements that I have just made and what happened to Job. God permits the devil to have such powers but Christ triumphs over the devil's schemes.

God strengthens us in the struggles and our tests become our testimonies. My mom had taken a small daily devotional book with her into hospital on the 25th of November 2019 and, when I found it in her small hospital bag, the tag was on the pages dated 15th and 16th October 2019. I read those pages and knew that my mom had wanted me to see them about spiritual warfare. I knew God was speaking to me, confirming what had happened to Clint and me and I just wept. God speaks to us all the time – we just need to learn how to listen!

25 November 2018 – Sunday

Clint woke up early, extremely worried and angry about who had moved and closed his laptop. He was shocked that he was still alive and could not figure it out. He had also laid in the car in the garage outstretched the previous night, waiting for God to take him, yet here he was, still alive and breathing. Clint was going through his own battle and said it felt like he had tried his best to convince us about the right way and for us to follow Jesus as He was the only way.

> **John 14:6**
> *Jesus said to him, "I am the way, the truth, and the life. No one comes to the Father except through Me.*

He said it felt at the time that his assignment was complete and, due to my lack of trust and paranoia and not believing what he was telling me about Jesus, he believed God was going to take him home. He was really tired and frustrated with us not believing him. He said all he wanted was for God to save our souls and to take his.

I am thankful today that Clint never gave up on us and kept trying his best to show his family the correct way, finally succeeding. He is the king, priest and prophet of his home today.

Accepting that it was not yet his time to go home, he decided to go for an early morning run, taking with him the two golden retrievers on their leads and letting our blind lab follow behind without a lead. He told Sharné and me to watch as our blind Labrador followed him. We both stood on the pavement watching as he sprinted up the road and we were both amazed at how Lexi was keeping up with him. We continued to watch as Clint turned right and Lexi turned left and, for a brief moment, we were both upset at what we were witnessing but then, in a blink of an eye, she turned around and started following him again. We watched until Clint and the dogs disappeared from our sight. It was incredible to witness the power of scent.

Clint had sent so many messages to his parents via WhatsApp for them to join us for a church service that morning. However, they were still very worried and deeply concerned about us, so they declined all his offers. We had promised Pastor Jonathan that we would join them at his church but things did not work out as planned. Clint and I were ready to head off to church when I realised that Lexi was nowhere to be found. I searched the garden and asked Clint where she was. He could not even remember that he had gone for a run with her without a lead and was quite shocked that she was now missing. Driving to church, we put a notice on the community neighbourhood watch WhatsApp group requesting assistance in locating our missing, black, blind Labrador.

When we reached the church site, we couldn't see any building resembling a church. We had a picture of a church in our minds. We now realise that we are the Church and that any building can be used for the gathering of the saints. I read the words 'Molly's Place' on the building and I told Clint this couldn't be the right place. Molly had been a nickname I had inherited from my friends years ago. We tried calling the Pastor to confirm the location but we were already running late because of the drama with Lexi so he was already preaching and unable to take our call. Feeling deflated, we drove back home. I recall feeling uneasy as Clint drove us home, scared he was going to do something to us, like drive us into oncoming traffic. Of course, he had no intention of doing that but, because of the persistent doubt and paranoia the demons were feeding me, it felt real.

Clint dropped off Sharné at Hayfields Mall so she could work and I lay down totally exhausted as I was beyond tired, but totally thankful that I had no injuries from the accident the previous day. Clint told me he had completed the 24-hour accident report which he hadn't. He said he thought he had done so. I told him again about the 10 Commandments – specifically the one which says "Honour your mother and father". I told him to please cancel our London trip as my mom had forbidden me to go. I said I had to be obedient to her and follow the commandment. He said he had cancelled our trip to London, but he hadn't.

Ephesians 6:2
"Honor your father and mother," which is the first commandment with promise.

On the WhatsApp neighbourhood group chat someone posted that they had found our black dog, Lexi. Strangely enough, our good friends live in the same road where she was found, which may have triggered Clint to send Hazel a very strange message:

> "Release Lexi now or I will release Roger's power on Rafa, you don't want to go there unless you are prepared to sacrifice your family. Please Hazel, let's do it the right way".

The two tennis fans had been rivals for years, whilst Clint supported Roger, Hazel supported Rafa, so this may have sparked the conversation which, as simple as it was, changed our friendship dynamics completely. Hazel could not come to terms with it and hasn't understood to this day what actually happened to us. I'm not sure what she believes regarding what we told her later about the spiritual warfare we experienced. I have since realised that only God can open people's eyes and ears to the truth and we cannot do it in our own strength no matter how hard we try. He will work in His own way and in His perfect timing.

Isaiah 55:8
"For My thoughts are not your thoughts, Nor are your ways My ways," says the Lord.

I must, however, add that God has an amazing sense of humour because, fast forward just over a year after this and guess what... Sharné won a prize to attend a tennis match in Cape Town and off went Hazel and Clint to watch their tennis stars – live – their tennis rivals, Roger and Rafa. Again, it just amazes me how the Lord Jesus Christ works out all things for the good of those that love Him.

Sharné had called Clint to fetch her early from work as she felt like she was having a nervous breakdown. My poor child was dealing with so much and she was leaving for Australia that evening to visit my sister. Clint didn't fetch her. For my husband, this was TOTALLY out of his character. His girls are his life. Sharné had to eventually ask her friend Rachel to fetch her. There was a battle raging in Clint's mind at that time. On one hand, he wanted to fetch his daughter but on the other hand, the enemy was telling him to leave her; the spirit of deception was confusing him. He knew he had to start installing discipline and order in his home but he knew he could no longer always be at the beck and call of his children. However, not even worrying how she would make her way home again shows how the enemy was manipulating the situation and him as well.

When Sharné arrived home, Clint asked her, Rachel and Rob to go with him to fetch Lexi. Clint proceeded to pray over Kyle's and Hazel's home and their dogs with Rachel, Rob and Sharné watching from the car. Around 40 minutes later, Clint sent Hazel another strange message:

> "Game set match Federer the ultimate GOAT debate is closed the greatest of all time has finally been solved in the spirit world Rafa has bowed down and submitted to this legend Roger, Rafa was a great competitor but everyone now knows the real GOAT and that is God of Love who is Roger Federer and who is Clint Mey when you see Clint Mey you will see Roger and people will then see God through Clint, great match finally you are now set free".

I try to imagine what must be going through someone's head when reading this, having known this person sending this message since childhood. Our friends said they had been too scared to come to our house during this time and, to this day, I have no idea what they thought was going on in our home.

I lay on our bed and, when I woke up a few moments later, I

felt a wet patch on my dress. It felt as if something had had sex with me. I couldn't get my head around it and still have no idea what took place. I believe things like this do happen to people and that demons can actually do this to humans, as crazy as it sounds.

Clint insisted that we baptise our three dogs. We had to get them into the pool and each of them had to have a ball in their mouth before he would allow Sharné to be taken to the airport to catch her flight to Australia. I was now naked and Clint said I should wear some clothes but I insisted that God had said "come as you are" earlier that morning. I wanted to go to church naked, much to Sharné's horror and rightfully so. I kept interpreting "Come as you are" literally and wanted to apply this as He had created us naked; thus, we must be naked and unashamed.

That was the enemy planting absolute rubbish in my head. Sharné was sobbing, just wanting to finish her packing for Australia. Poor Lexi was terrified of the water and she was so heavy that Sharné and I battled many times before eventually getting her into the water. Clint told Sharné that she would not go to Australia if we didn't get this right, complaining that our house was unruly and he was going to install order back into our lives. We spoke the words over our lives. We even wanted a personalized car number plate with 'Meyhem' on it. Now we fully understand the power of words and the tongue.
The Bible is very clear on that.

> **Proverbs 18:21**
> *Death and life are in the power of the tongue, And those who love it will eat its fruit.*
>
> **James 3:5**
> *Even so the tongue is a little member and boasts*

great things. See how great a forest a little fire kindles!

We eventually got it right – all three dogs in the pool, each with a ball in their mouths, Clint baptised them and Sharné was able to finish her packing. I don't think she could have left the house any sooner. God's timing is always perfect. She really needed to get out of our house and being with my sister was the perfect place for her. Sharné was extremely affected by what was going on even though she didn't understand it and, to this very day, dislikes talking about it as it was such a petrifying time for our girls. I stood by the front door saying my goodbyes to her and Clint.

Clint then told me I could ring the bell in the kitchen and cry out to my father to end the game. Clint was referring to our Heavenly Father. The little blue bell on our kitchen windowsill reads 'ring for dads help'. I was confused by this and sat in the lounge. A few moments later, frantically begging for the game to end, I rang the bell as instructed. This didn't seem to help at all. I had no cellphone and I can't remember how I found Clint's parents' number, but I called them, using our home landline. I must have called my sister in Johannesburg to get their number, as hers was the only one I knew offhand.

I told Clint's dad that something was very wrong and I was worried about Clint. I took down notes, as he told me to rebuke satan out of Clint. They knew he had unclean spirits, evident from his behaviour.

I have that note and what is incredible to see is that, as I read the note, there are very powerful words missing. Clearly, the demons did not want me to write down the most powerful Name, the Name above every name, Jesus.

The note read:

> "Pray for Clint. I rebuke satin in the name of ....
> Demon be gone I command you leave in the name of
> ...."

Jesus Himself said that in His Name you will cast out demons.

> **Philippians 2:9-11**
> *⁹Therefore God also has highly exalted Him and given Him the name which is above every name, ¹⁰that at the name of Jesus every knee should bow, of those in heaven, and of those on earth, and of those under the earth, ¹¹and that every tongue should confess that Jesus Christ is Lord, to the glory of God the Father.*
>
> **Romans 14:11**
> *For it is written: "As I live, says the Lord, Every knee shall bow to Me, and every tongue shall confess to God."*
>
> **Mark 16:17**
> *And these signs will follow those who believe: In My name they will cast out demons…*

Linda, my sister, was also very confused and worried about what was going on with us, but totally grateful that her niece was getting out of the mess. Clint had been speaking to her from the airport and he kept telling her that our dad, who had passed away some years ago, was keeping him in stitches.

Months later, Clint's mom told us that my mom had called her, worried about Sharné being in the car with Clint that afternoon when he drove her to the airport. She told Clint's mom he had an empty suitcase and a pocket of cement in the back of his car which he didn't. She said my mom told her she was scared that Clint was going to chop Sharné up into pieces and put her into the suitcase with the cement and throw her into the sea. When my mom told me that her spirit was involved in our warfare, I really didn't understand how much the enemy was manipulating and plaguing my mom's and Clint's mom's minds with lies. Clint's mom was scared for her own life as Clint had told his own mom not to contact my mom or he would have to kill her. But she said she spoke to my mom constantly as they were so worried about us.

When Clint got back from the airport and told me that my dad, who had passed away a few years earlier, had kept him in stitches the whole way home, he said, "Your dad has such a great sense of humour". He could barely contain himself with all the laughter, trying to speak in between fits of laughter.

I told him I had rung the bell as he had instructed but nothing had happened. I then asked him if I could see the footage on our CCTV cameras of the outer area where his belt and pants were lying because that's where he had left them when getting in the pool with the dogs but my mind was telling me other things. I was convinced that he had been up to something earlier, possibly because he had told me he wasn't able to fetch Sharné from work as he was having tea with a female friend of ours, which was an absolute lie, but I believed every word. He fumbled around, not being able to open the code for the security cameras. This made me even more alarmed. The devil was playing games with my mind yet again and I was falling for it hook, line and sinker and Clint was feeding this monster. He proceeded to tell me that he had had affairs with six women and he named them. He also told me that Ntombi, our domestic worker, was his soul mate. Satan was feeding him with lies and I was soaking it all in. Of course, none of this was true. Clint said he knew he was lying at the time but he wanted to feed my paranoia. He couldn't believe that I believed all this and found it amusing as to how stupid the devil actually is.

When the Lord tells us that he (satan) is the father of all lies, He was certainly not joking about it. We experienced this firsthand in so many instances over the past few days. Satan and his demons wanted to hurt us and they were assigned to break up our marriage and to destroy the course that God had planned for us. BUT GOD had other plans. Having no joy in watching the footage on the verandah, I then asked Clint to show me the cancelled air tickets and our bank statements. But he couldn't open either of the applications on his computer; nothing was working.

I started rebuking satan out of him and he threw me down in the study, rebuking satan out of me. It's an absolute miracle that, as he threw me onto the couch in the study, my head did not hit the sharp edge of the shelf above. Clint told me much later he felt something enter him when he threw me down. He said it felt as if he had swallowed something. He said it was like a deep shift in his soul, something not easy to describe. I was petrified and wanted to leave immediately. I wanted to go to Kelsey who was staying at her friend's house. They lived close by so I knew I could walk there.

I quickly rushed to my room and opened the top cupboard to retrieve a suitcase which contained all our important documents such as passports, kids' reports, immunisation cards and other items that I had collected over the years. The suitcase was heavy – very heavy. I have no idea where I got the strength from but I pulled it down and it smashed the stool I was standing on. I dragged the bag down the passage and Clint came after me, grabbing me around the neck and throwing me down. I honestly thought he was going to kill me. The only telephone number I knew off by heart, as mentioned earlier, was my sister's in Johannesburg. I called her frantically on our landline from the study.

I told her what had just happened to me and she said she would drive down from Johannesburg the next day. Clint locked all the doors and then he locked the interior security gate in our passage and took all the keys with him. He then picked up the other phone which was in our bedroom and started playing gospel music. My sister told him he was being very rude as we couldn't hear each other. He told her not to come to Pietermaritzburg but she insisted that she would. Soon thereafter, Clint called Phil Gill who arrived shortly after I finished the call with my sister. He started praying in tongues over our house. Remembering at this stage I was not really familiar with this practice, I begged Phil to take me to Kelsey's friend's house as I just wanted to be with Kelsey. Phil sat down with us in the study and told Clint he was not behaving like a Christian. He spoke to both of us with words of encouragement and prayed with us before leaving. Clint had told Phil he had it all under control as he said he believed he had swallowed the demon that was in me.

I was still not happy that Clint could not show me any CCTV footage from earlier that day and started to think of all the women he said he had been with. I now know this was all a lie from the pit of hell, but, in that moment, I was filled with extreme jealousy and an overwhelming feeling that I wanted my husband back. I was thinking about the deodorant cans again that were always being placed around our home with *Playboy, Playgirl* and *Tropical*. I thought he was a playboy and I now wanted to know if he still had a desire for me.

It was like a power struggle. After thinking he was going to kill me, I now wanted to have sex with him. That itself is not normal behaviour. We were both filled with lust – probably the spirit of lust. We were wild and intimate until the early hours of the morning. It was supernatural. Clint kept saying over and over again that it was lust and not love.

26 November 2018 – Monday

Clint was up from the early hours of the morning clearing out his mailbox on his laptop. He hadn't been to work all week and, in his mind, felt we were still heading to London as planned the following day. He had checked us in even though he had promised that he'd cancelled the trip as my mom had forbidden me to go and Kelsey had also told us outright that she wasn't going with us. My mom, as I have mentioned before, just knew something was wrong with us and her own spirit was involved in this warfare. She told us in discussions much later that strange things were happening to her as well. The enemy was planting seeds in her mind that Clint was in heavy financial debt, involved in gambling and was a drug lord and murderer – again all lies.

Clint has been nothing but a loving, kind son-in-law to her for over 24 years. It's quite frightening to think the enemy can have such power over people's minds. She was absolutely terrified of what was going on and had no way of helping us as she was stuck in Amber Valley, Howick with no means of transport. She felt so helpless and said this had truly aged her. We now know that God was in control all the time.

Romans 8:28
And we know that all things work together for good to those who love God, to those who are the called according to His purpose.

Clint told me that morning he was able to see into the future. He showed me stuff on his phone, saying he had already seen some events happening that day.

Clint became my dead dad on this particular day. As crazy as it sounds, that's exactly what happened. We now understand that most certainly was not my dad, but a soul copy. We studied this further nearly two years later and I will talk about it again at a later stage but, for now, I will relay the events of what happened on this particular day.

Every Monday I go to Des, my physio, for therapy on my arm for tennis elbow. That morning, Clint contacted Des, telling her I would be unable to keep the appointment as I had one with my dad, John Collin Moffett. When listening to his voice note a few weeks later, I could hear that he was talking in the third person and not as Clint. He also told her Clint and Mary-Ann were travelling to London the next day. The next time I spoke to Des, she said she had found the voice note extremely strange as she knew my dad had passed away a few years prior. Clint also phoned my sister-in-law, Wendy, telling her he was John Collin Moffett which she found totally bizarre. Then he called my sister, Gillian, who was traveling from Johannesburg with James and Emily. He told her to bring milk and bananas.

He told Gillian he needed lots of milk and bananas. Clint said my mom loved bananas, which she did, and that my dad wasn't allowed to eat them, which he wasn't because of the high potassium in them. My mom used to have a big sign in the banana bowl DON'T EAT. My dad loved milk and drank it daily and my mom hated milk and never drank a glass. Clint had also sent me a message a few days prior asking me who had made my dad go bananas, he wanted to know if it was Brenda (my mom), me or my dads first wife.

Clint went off to *Builders Warehouse* that morning to collect some sand as the gardener needed extra to complete some paving work. He said the man behind the counter had told him he would also need cement to bind the families back together, so he took a 40 kg bag of cement, thinking there was a lot of work to be done within the family. Clint said my dad had told him the families were falling apart and order needed to be restored. Sadly, after years of marriage, both my sisters were contemplating divorce at this stage. My one sister had only told me a few days prior about her marriage troubles but at that stage I was already in full blown spiritual warfare and thus unable to provide the support she needed. I also hadn't even mentioned it to Clint.

Gillian arrived from Johannesburg that morning and said she was shocked when she saw me. By not eating and sleeping properly for days, I must have been a sight for sore eyes. She walked in with the milk and bananas as instructed by Clint and said whenever the word 'banana' was mentioned, I went a little crazy. I knew something was wrong but I didn't know what it was. I told my sister about the 'ritual' at the Meys' house on the Friday evening and how Clint and I had stood in the middle of the circle as the people spoke some things which I had not understood. Today, I fully understand and know that they were all trying to help us – but they were not deliverance ministers and were not equipped to deal with something like this.

I also told her we had a pastor come around a few times and that Phil had come to the house the previous night and prayed in another language over our home. I was scared and confused and truly did not trust a single person. It's hard to explain the fear and paranoia. I told her Ntombi and Clint may be poisoning me and I think all this talk got my sister's back up against the Meys and Clint. She was so confused and scared herself, having no idea what was going on. The way her baby sister was reacting was worrying her. She was practically my mother while we were growing up and watched over me for years in boarding school. Our bond had always been extremely strong. I called a friend from work that morning, asking him if he thought I was going mad. I asked him to tell my sister about the number plate I had seen (Uriel).

Gillian and Emily then began to burn sage as they walked around the house, also saying things I didn't understand. They said it was a cleansing ritual for our home. To this day, I am not exactly sure what ritual that was, but it appeared to be a new age practice called 'sage smudging'.

I was truly thankful they had driven down for me. I needed help and no-one seemed to be able to provide the relief from the constant torture and onslaught in my mind; the constant feeling of anguish in the pit of my stomach. I could barely string a proper sentence together. Looking back, I keep trying to understand it all and how demons can take over our bodies; that some things we see on horror movies actually do happen to ordinary people in real life. The spirit realm is real and when we dabble in the dark, we can expect to get burnt. God puts us through a fiery furnace for a reason. God's Word says we do not choose God but that He chooses us. I thank Him often for choosing us.

> **John 15:16**
> *You did not choose Me, but I chose you and appointed you that you should go and bear fruit, and that your fruit should remain, that whatever you ask the Father in My name He may give you.*

Clint and I often look back and thank Him for what He

allowed us to experience together and, as scary as it was, we wouldn't change it for anything.

James and my sister, Gillian, had made an appointment for Clint and me with the Brent Black Group. They were an addiction recovery support service provider, offering specialist counselling for drug addiction, alcoholism and behavioral disorders as well as counselling for general social-emotional wellbeing. My family had no idea what was going on with us and they thought we had possibly been given something at the braai we had attended the previous week or that we were on some kind of drugs. Some friends later said that is exactly what they had also thought – mushrooms, LSD – you name it. But one thing I can promise is that we were on no drugs whatsoever and, for those who know us and know us well, they will vouch that we would not lie about things like this.

Clint refused to come to the appointment as he wanted us to all join him for a meeting at my mother's house. He said my dad wanted a meeting with all of us and that John Collin Moffett had a scheduled appointment at 3:30 pm with God and some guests. He told us he needed us all to be present. He told us to come with the milk and bananas. He became very worked up and angry that we were not listening to him, saying he thought he was failing the request. He said he was being derailed – exactly how I had been feeling over the past few days. He drove up to my mom's house and was refused entry at security as my mom had called them requesting that he be denied access. He threw his car keys at Percy, the security guard, who was on duty at the time, as well as his wallet, and told him he could have it. He said the family thought it was all about money, but it was actually all about love. He lay down under a tree at the entrance gate of Amber Valley and said he felt he was in the garden of Eden.

That day, he sent so many messages to so many people, one after the other – Sharné, Kelsey, James, Emily, work colleagues and others. I know Clint he could never type so fast and so accurately. I could tell that something supernatural was typing those messages. Clint was definitely oppressed by demonic spirits.

Months later, when listening back to his voice notes, one could hear it wasn't him. He also went from being calm to very angry and stressed because no-one was listening. He angrily spoke in the third person, claiming we were all disobedient and we were embarrassing my dad.

Kelsey, along with James, Gillian and Emily, came with me to meet Brent Black. I remember my speech was very bad. I couldn't pronounce the place we were going to, namely Armitage Road. As I begged Clint to join us, I felt I was also being derailed once again. Brent Black did a drug test, the result of which was negative, and the blood tests from the Friday all came back negative as well. That is because there were no drugs involved in this. It was spiritual warfare.

I tried to explain what was going on and I think he probably thought I was mad and going through some sort of mental breakdown. He made a call and requested that I go to Oatlands Centre the following morning. Clint didn't arrive but continued to send messages in the third person, faster than he could ever type and his messages looked as if they were being sent by a madman.

He arrived home at dusk, close to 6 pm, and rang the gate bell frantically. I ran down the passage and pressed the button to open the gate so he could enter, but I had no idea he had then used his remote to open the gate himself and now the gate was closing on his car.

He was so excited to tell us that he now knew what it was all about. It was about hearts and thumbs, he said. He tried to tell my sister but she wasn't hearing any of it. Clint got out the car and James was so angry that he hadn't come to the appointment which James had kindly arranged and paid for. With Clint carrying on about my dad or something (I can't really remember all the details), James threw down his phone, charged towards Clint and proceeded to head-butt and punch him in the face. Clint went flying into the doorway, smashing and breaking our picture frame that hung against the wall. Clint called out "Jesus, help me!". He said he didn't feel a thing – no pain whatsoever even though his nose was dislocated and he was bleeding profusely as he lay on the grass, in a crucified position, with our two golden retrievers on either side of him. Kelsey was frantically crying and jumped over the wall to the neighbour's house. Kelsey had been traumatised by the whole experience and, on occasions when she came home to pop in for clothes, she prayed so beautifully for me. Thank you for all your prayers, Kels.

Emily called an ambulance and they arrived a short while later. Clint went from thinking he was Rudolf the Red-Nosed Reindeer, because his nose was swollen and all bandaged up, to thinking he was the Grinch of Christmas. We all just shouted "take him away". Shame – how terrible – but at the time, we didn't know what else to do. Clint said that, as he sat in the ambulance chatting to the paramedic, he asked him to tell him about Christmas and the elves. The man told him that only one of the Christmas elves had a proper name – *Sugarplum Mary*. Clint said he thought about me and all the messages he had sent me about keeping the elf nourished. He was always trying to feed me, saying the elf must remain nourished during our warfare.

When he arrived at the hospital, he told the nursing staff

that he only had two requests. Firstly, he wanted a full blood transfusion, but every drop had to be the Blood of Jesus. Secondly, he wanted them to send their strongest doctor. When a male African doctor finally arrived at his bedside, he said, "Samson – they sent you" because he looked so strong and mighty. He was a short, stocky and very muscular man.

I had begged James to take me to the hospital to drop off a bag which I had packed for Clint and he was not happy about that at all. I continued begging and insisting until eventually he agreed. When Clint was lying on the grass earlier, he had told me that James and my sister were the wolves in sheep's clothing. When I saw Clint lying in the hospital bed with his arms outstretched, praying over the people, I told James that Clint even looked like my dad, which he did to me. James told me to be quiet and not say anything else in order for Clint to remain calm. Clint said that, during his time in the casualty, he was lying in his bed praying over the sick and he had a sudden feeling that he needed to change his shirt. He said it felt like his power of praying had something to do with his neon shirts, so he quickly changed and continued praying.

He would feel the power as he prayed over the people, showing them hearts and thumbs. He believed it was a blood war. After dropping off the bag with Clint, we headed home, stopping at the petrol station. I sat in the back seat and asked my sister if she was the wolf in sheep's clothing. She started crying. I can't blame her. What a terrible thing to ask someone who loves you and has just driven hours to come and help you. We both cried that night and I pray that one day she will understand how real spiritual demonic forces can attack one's lives and that I had really no reason to ask that at all. Seeds had been planted and the enemy was laughing.

When we arrived home, we realised there was nothing to eat and everyone wanted KFC. I asked James to please not buy me anything spicy as I had sores all over my tongue and mouth. Gillian, Emily and Kelsey asked for KFC burgers. I remember, when James came back, he had only bought Gillian and Emily the burgers and guess what he bought us… spicy, hot chicken! Kelsey couldn't believe it. He told her KFC had run out of chicken, so he had to go to another chicken outlet. Kelsey still questioned him which KFC outlet it was that had no more chicken.

The very next day, Kelsey said she went and asked that same KFC outlet if they had run out of chicken the previous evening and they said they hadn't. I keep saying the same thing – the spirit world is very real and sometimes we don't understand how it works. James himself will not even know why he decided to buy hot, spicy chicken that night, but the enemy sure did. The enemy can manipulate situations by using people to his advantage to continue to cause harm.

I was extremely paranoid that night and I wouldn't let James sleep in the lounge by himself. Everything seemed out of order. Things were strange and I felt threatened and scared. My sister had spilt something in her toiletry bag and everything was lying on the kitchen draining board, which was very disturbing to me. It was as if things were being moved around to confuse me and I watched everyone's moves. Even Kelsey said she was aware of a feeling of uneasiness and was also acutely aware of things constantly being shifted and moved around – the bananas Gillian had bought and Halls lozenges that Clint had bought. Thinking that each team member would have a pack at the meeting which never happened, Clint said he was extremely excited to see who would choose the Extra strong flavour, as that would be a powerful player. He said he was told by my dad to buy them as my dad had told Clint there was going to be a lot of talking involved that day so that we could resolve all the family issues and therefore we would need them. They were left lying on the kitchen counter.

Clint also said that God had told him it would be a very busy and long day and, at the end of it, if all went according to plan, he would be on his knees in the kitchen fighting for me, his wife. Unfortunately, he was fighting for his life in the ICU.

Kelsey slept at home that night with me and I was grateful to have James, Gillian and Emily there too.

The parking ticket found in Clint's car on 23 November 2018

You've got a new story to write. And it looks nothing like your past.

The picture Clint showed me that was on his phone on 12 November 2018

Kelseys artwork in her room with a Dandelion and the words:
Just Breathe
referred to on 17 November 2018

Meeting Roger Federer – March 2017

The photo that disturbed Clint on 23 November 2018 – wanting to know where the wife was?

The photo that I showed Clint on 24 November 2018 – now included the wife

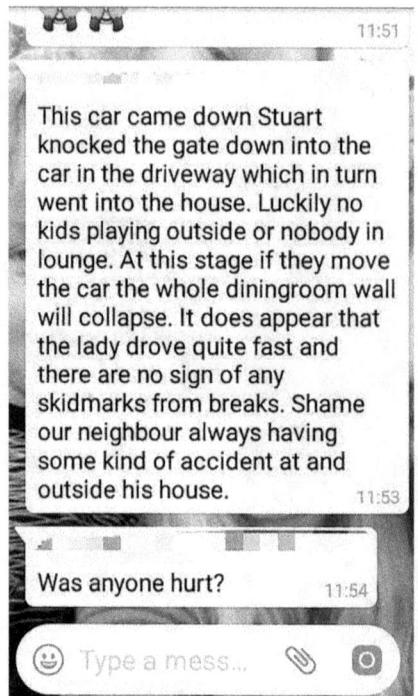

The Whats Up message on 24 November 2018 from the group chat, later sent to me by "Kyle" in December 2018

The Whats Up message sent to "Hazel" on 25 November 2018

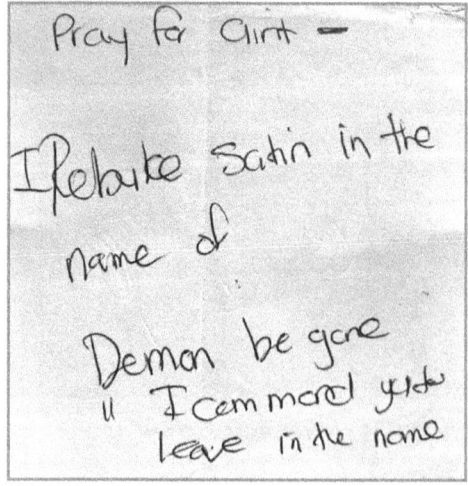

Original note referred to from the 25 November 2018

Our family – from left to right: Sharne Mey, Kelsey Mey, Mary-Ann Mey and Clint Mey

Confirmation I got to write this book

Our faithful, loyal family friends... Luca, Lexi and Charlie

Chapter 5

Reflection Time

27 November 2018 – Tuesday

Clint had been sent to ICU that night. Prior to this, he had had no heart trouble or any blood pressure issues. As a 10-times Comrades Marathon runner, he has been blessed with good health, but on this evening, his blood pressure was going crazy. The devil tried to take him out, BUT GOD! He spent the next few days at Medi-Clinic Hospital until he was later transferred to Akeso Clinic. He told me that, during his stay at Medi-Clinic, he was not himself, doing crazy, bizarre things like splashing the hand sanitiser everywhere and saying it was the Blood of Jesus. He said he felt that he needed to keep the demons away. He believed he was under attack and wanted the Blood of Jesus to cover him. He had accused his mom of molesting him and she said she nearly died of embarrassment. You can just imagine a mom who has loved her son her whole life, never having harmed a hair on his head, trying to cope and deal with such shocking and devastating lies, especially to be accused of this in front of the entire ward filled with patients and nurses who were staring at her in disgust.

He then told his mom he had made a mistake and it wasn't her that had molested him, but Mary-Ann's granddad who had molested Mary-Ann. Clint's mom said they had told her in the hospital that, if she couldn't calm her son down, he would need to be admitted to Town Hill Mental Hospital.

To go to hospital for a dislocated nose from a head-butt and punch and land up in ICU is just not heard of and, quite frankly, a clear indication of how the devil tries to take one out. They ran a series of blood tests, drug tests and all kinds of other tests. They did a CT scan as well as an MRI scan while he was in hospital, all of which were clear. There were no drugs in his system and there was no detection of any abnormal brain activity.

That morning, my bag was packed and I was ready to be taken to Oatlands Care Centre, a place I had never heard of before. My sister told me it was in Howick and she had heard it was a lovely place. I was terribly confused and scared, not really understanding what was going on with me. I didn't fight it and kept on thinking about Bible school. I have no idea why. I was unsettled the entire car ride. Paranoia and fear continued to grip me. My mind was racing, trying to put it all together, which I couldn't – not at that stage.

On our way to Howick, we paid a visit to Clint's parents. There was a lot of tension in the air as no-one really understood what was going on. Gillian asked Clint's parents a few times which cult they were part of and what ritual they had performed the previous Friday night. She was honestly so concerned for me and, when I explained to her what had happened, I myself didn't even realise that they were just trying to help us through prayer. My sister again said every time milk and bananas were mentioned, I changed. I was still extremely paranoid and trusted no-one.

Arriving at Oatlands was terrifying. I sat quietly with Emily as she completed the necessary forms. I took a photo of all the rules. There seemed to be so many and I remember being overwhelmed. How was I possibly going to remember them all? When I asked about the rules, they told me each person had a copy on their bedside table so I shouldn't worry about trying to remember them. At this stage, my sister was taking a look around the facility. After all the documents were completed, my sister walked me to my room. My roommate was standing there to greet me. The first thing Gillian noticed was a huge wooden cross hanging around her neck with the inscription *'John 3:16'* on it. I had told my sister that was the only verse I was told to read and highlight in the Bible. I had not yet seen the necklace but I was tearful and the last thing I said to my sister was that I now knew how my dad must have felt when we left him at the frail care centre a few years prior because of his partial dementia.

I remembered how he had cried during our first few visits which was extremely upsetting. It's gut-wrenching seeing your grown dad crying, something I had never witnessed before as he just wanted to go home. He was desperate to be back in his own home and now I also just wanted to go home.

Gillian said she cried when she drove off heading back to Johannesburg, hoping she had done the right thing by leaving me there. Yes, Gillian, you did the right thing by leaving me there and I can never thank you and the family enough. Thank you, my beautiful sister!

I had no idea of what lay ahead of me and quite frankly just wanted to be by myself. At my first lunch, I sat down at a table by myself and my roommate approached me. That is when I first saw the big wooden cross with *'John 3:16'* written on it. I burst out crying and felt extremely stressed as my dad's name was John and I recalled all the times Clint had made me read that verse. It was the only verse in the Bible he wanted me to read. I now know he was making doubly sure that I knew the truth as the devil came in with so many lies. Looking back now, it was probably because it is the most important verse in the Bible – the gospel in a nutshell. Clint really wanted me to know that Jesus died for us, every single one of us, and we must just believe in Jesus for salvation.

> **Acts 4:12**
> *Nor is there salvation in any other, for there is no other name under heaven given among men by which we must be saved.*

I didn't really want to talk to anybody but I was introduced to a 'David' (my brother's name). I was thus drawn to him and spent most of my meals talking to David, learning more about him and his family. Over the next few days, I slowly started opening up to him. I also recall an 'Ntombi' (our domestic worker's name). Where Clint was staying in Akeso, there was a 'Mary-Ann' and a 'Chloe-Mary', a rather unique name that he hadn't heard of before. It was rather ironic with all these familiar names at both the places we were at.

I recall there were a few Christians and I clearly remember the old lady who stayed in the room next to me because I had seen her and her daughter at *The Farmer's Daughter* the week prior. That felt extremely strange to me. She needed financial help and I recall feeling overwhelmed by all the needy people. I believed I had to be extremely cautious about who I would choose to assist financially in the future as many would come to decieve me. As I said, I trusted no-one at this stage. What were the chances of the very same people I had seen in a restaurant the week prior now being in the room next to me? This only made me more paranoid and added further stress. More blood tests were taken and every day they would take my temperature and blood pressure. All my vital signs were completely normal throughout my entire stay.

I was introduced to my psychiatrist – a very kind, gentle man. I began telling him everything that had been happening in our house over the past few days. He asked me numerous questions and I explained to him that, after giving my life to God, how my life had changed. I said it had started off with such beauty but then changed. I told him it was because I didn't know the Bible and relayed how Clint had been behaving. Through many tears, I told him everything that had happened to us.

I was still extremely uneasy and kept jumping up to look through his window. The doctor said he knew exactly what I was looking at – the ambulance and specifically the angel wings on it. I was amazed as that was exactly what I was looking at and drawing comfort from. Looking back now, I see just how amazing our God is and how His Hand was always there protecting me on my journey.

Jesus is in control now and always will be and I take such comfort in knowing that. God put a doctor in my life who had studied religion for seven years, so he knew exactly what I was talking about even though I didn't understand it at the time. He knew all about spiritual warfare and the fight for our souls. I was so thankful he did not prescribe me any medication – NOTHING!!!! – Any other doctor would have thought I was totally crazy and had completely lost my mind with all these bizarre stories and probably would have heavily sedated me. THANK YOU, JESUS! This was also the third time drug tests were being done and of course they all came back negative. This was no drug. This was full-blown spiritual warfare.

> **Psalm 119:71**
> *It is good for me that I have been afflicted, that I may learn Your statutes.*

The only 'prescription' the doctor wrote down on a piece of paper was a list of the following books I needed to read: *This Present Darkness, Celebration of Discipline* and *Julian of Norwich*. I still have that piece of paper.

Over the next few days, I was trying to come to terms with what had happened to Clint and me. I did not trust Clint. I seriously thought he had poisoned me, tried to brainwash me, cast spells on me and had powers over me because I saw him switching lights on and off on demand and because of all the strange and terrible things that had happened. We only fully understood what had happened to us weeks later and we still look back at that time with utter amazement. We may never fully understand or know why it happened to us but we are thankful every day that it did.

There were a few strange things that upset me during my stay at Oatlands and that played on my mind a lot:

My door beanbag did not match my door number. It had '12' on it and there were big red arrows all over pointing to room 12. I felt like I was being called to room 12, but I never ever went as I felt it was temptation and I had to fight against it. I eventually asked them to take the doorstop away and, soon after asking what the red arrows were there for, they removed them from the pillars and walls.

Everyone receives rules next to their beds – everyone... but me. My bed was the only one that did not have the rules next to it and that disturbed me tremendously. I did not want to break the rules and I kept telling them I didn't have a set but no-one seemed to worry. I recall a visit from a close friend of mine. She had been drinking as I could smell it on her breath. I told her she was not allowed to visit if she had been drinking and she just laughed at me, saying, "Mary, stop panicking! You know I'm a rule breaker". It stressed me that I would be in trouble. The next time she visited me she was sober. My poor friend was trying to deal with her own struggles at the time and I am truly thankful that she took the time during such a difficult period in her life to visit me.

Every person there had a hardcovered blue file handed to them in which they kept all their notes and handouts, except me. I was the only one in the entire group to have a soft, flimsy yellow file. I wondered why I was different and it troubled me immensely. I felt like I was being targeted and watched closely by everyone. I was the odd one out. I also felt I was being tested constantly. Therefore, I didn't want to say much in the group sessions.

Our bathroom had a tile missing and on the cement was the inscription 'Genesis' with a picture of an elephant and a shrew. I looked at it all the time and found it strange, yet comforting. With one tile missing and behind it, a carved biblical inscription, I am sure that you would agree that was totally out of the ordinary.

My time spent at Oatlands felt strange. It was weird – I am unable to put it into words to describe it – the people, the doctors, the lecturers – all of it. I practically kept to myself, trusting no-one. I didn't join in on the movie nights, the games evenings or the walks to the shops. I alienated myself and avoided unnecessary social interaction. I spent most of my free time reading the gospel of John.

Chloe visited me one day and, as we sat outside, she said

something strange to me. She told me that, if this had been years ago, we would have both been burnt at the stake as they would have called us witches. I was certainly no witch but had clearly invited witchcraft into my life. Thankfully, my God is much more powerful than any witch or warlock.

I was grateful I had taken my small pink christening Bible which my grandmother had given me but, to my surprise, someone had left a Bible in my bedside drawer. Come to think of it now, the rules were missing for my stay at Oatlands but the most important rules I would need for the rest of my life were left behind in the drawer – the Holy Bible.

B asic
I nstructions
B efore
L eaving
E arth

God has an amazing way of showing us and revealing Himself to us – through His Word.

Matthew 24:35
Heaven and earth will pass away, but My words will by no means pass away.

I had started reading the Gospel of John, where my sister, Linda, had told me to start. Little did I know that Clint's dad had taken him a small book to read at Akeso. It was the Gospel of John which he was now also reading. It was the first time as an adult that Clint was now reading the Word of God.

One evening, I called Charmaine and Phil, requesting them not to visit Clint. I truly didn't trust them and thought they were involved in what we were experiencing, especially after Phil had left me alone with Clint even though I had begged him to take me to Tracey's house to stay with Kelsey. I apologised for my behaviour much later and felt so ashamed that I had ever doubted their intentions. But Phil knew all about spiritual warfare and all was forgotten and forgiven. They are a truly blessed and kind couple whom the Lord put in our path.

I was also upset with Clint's parents as I was looking back, questioning why they hadn't come to our home to help us. None of our friends came either but now I fully understand that they were all terrified of us and couldn't understand what was going on. Clint's mom told me she had forbidden his dad to come to us as she genuinely thought Clint would kill him and I learnt months later that even my brother's wife, Wendy, had told my brother he could not fly down to help us as he was not equipped to do so. Friends said they drove past our house but were too scared to come in. God also keeps people away. One thing I have learnt on this journey is how God opens and closes doors.

I recall when Clint's parents came to visit me at Oatlands one afternoon. I was very uneasy and asked his dad not to wave his hands in front of me like a magician all the time. It was the exact same movement Clint had been showing me and I did not fully understand why it was making me feel so on edge. Clint had told me he was the greatest magician and his dad was the greatest illusionist. They had both been very intrigued with magic and illusion over the years. Clint's parents gave me the news that his brother's ex-wife had just had a car accident the day before and I felt as if something dark was happening. I didn't trust them and wanted to be left on my own. I probably appeared very offish and distant.

The week had gone by quickly and the people at Oatlands were excited for their outing. We were all going to a farm for horse therapy. We travelled by bus to a beautiful farm in the countryside. The anxious feeling in the pit of my stomach had still not eased. It was worse than anything I have ever felt. This feeling was intensifying and had been with me for days. The fight for my soul continued to rage on.

I still did not trust anyone and, on this particular day, my anxiety and nervousness kicked in big time. I truly felt I was going to be murdered out there on the farm by these strangers and they were going to use the horses to do it. We walked some distance before going into a field where very few horses could actually be seen in the distance but, before I knew it, horses started making their way to all of us – a beautiful sight to see. These powerful creatures parading themselves in front of us were excited to see all the people. They seemed to be drawn to us.

I was terribly nervous to touch the horse closest to me and deep down I was hoping the horse would ease this feeling I was unable to shake off. Someone had sent me a video the day before of horses being used in a hospital to assist the patient's therapy, so I guess I was hoping for the same result but this was not the case. I walked about the field keeping a safe distance but, every now and again, I took a chance and stretched out my hand to touch the horses. It was really the most amazing thing watching so many horses appear out of what seemed like nowhere. Everyone had a wonderful experience and, even though I was not fully relaxed, I was grateful for the opportunity and I would really love to go back there one day.

As I climbed into bed that night, tears streamed down my face. I clearly remember calling out to God to please help me and take away this terrible feeling in my stomach. I was desperate. I was still reading the Gospel of John.

Psalm 30:2
O Lord my God, I cried out to You, And You healed me.

I woke up the next morning and the feeling was gone – thank You, Lord. I could hardly believe it. I felt different but I was still confused about what had happened to us.

Over the next few days, I began feeling more like myself again. I was reading my Bible, going for an early morning daily walk around the property and started opening up to people a bit more. I also started taking more care of myself and putting on a bit of makeup. I received a few visitors during my stay – some friends and some family. My mom and brother also paid me a visit. I continued to see the doctor and psychologist and, in the evenings, Clint and I would catch up, sometimes speaking on the phone for ages.

We had agreed he would stay at a B&B for a few days so I could get my head around what was going on. On 7th December 2018, Chloe fetched me on her way home from work and I was able to spend the weekend at their home in Hilton. She had arranged for us to go horse-riding on the Saturday morning which was very sweet of her. Thereafter she drove me home so I could spend a few hours there. She knew I was struggling to make sense of it all. We saw Clint for a few minutes before he left. He said he felt very uneasy being around Chloe for some strange reason. I think he believed Chloe wanted me to go to England with her as she was planning on leaving her husband and moving there. Clint felt threatened by her and the influence he thought she had on me at the time. While we stood in the kitchen, Chloe tried to look up the medication, which the doctor had prescribed for Clint, on her cellphone – medication which he refused to take. As she typed the name of the medication, her phone went blank and switched off. It had nothing to do with the battery life. She tried to reboot it and put in her password but it wouldn't accept the code. She tried again and realised she would have to go home as, if she entered an incorrect code again, it would block her sim card. I told her that was exactly what had happened to my phone and my phone had also been doing strange things. I told her it seemed my phone had been taken over supernaturally.

Chloe left and I spent some time with our dogs. Just being back home was nice. Days prior to me going to Oatlands, I can honestly say our dogs were wild. It was as if they were not our dogs. Their behaviour was different and I recall one day when Luca jumped on our bed and attacked me – totally out of character. I truly believe even animals can have demons attached to them. I guess this is true because Jesus himself cast out 2 000 demons and sent them into pigs.

>**Matthew 8:31**
>*So the demons begged Him, saying, "If You cast us out, permit us to go away into the herd of swine."*

Chloe fetched me a few hours later and we spent the evening chatting and watching TV. The next day, my sister Gillian told me that Clint had not wanted her to drive down from Johannesburg. He had tried to persuade her to stay home but when she insisted that she was driving down, he then told her to bring R10 000. I immediately asked Clint about that and he denied it. My sister sent me a screenshot of the message Clint had sent her. I was really struggling with what to believe. The devil will use all kinds of tactics to try and destroy relationships. Clint truly did not remember sending that message to my sister, probably because he actually didn't, but the demon in him at the time did.

I was so thankful for my weekend away and, early Monday morning, Chloe drove me back to Oatlands. My family wanted me to stay longer but I felt ready to go home and the doctor agreed. My doctor had also had discussions with Clint's doctor at Akeso and Clint had already been discharged.

On the day I left Oatlands, Kyle had offered to fetch Sharné from the airport as she was returning from Australia and Kelsey was also looking forward to coming home. I had missed my girls so much and could not wait to see them and spend time with them. The girls also wanted Clint to stay in the B&B so he agreed and spent about one week there during which time we frequently visited each other even though our kids didn't want us to as they were scared.

Clint and I were both trying to understand what we had just been through and we both felt like we were now back on earth. It was a soft, gentle landing. For both of us to go through this supernatural experience at the same time was incredible and something we will never put behind us. We often talk about it even to this day. God allowed us to experience something to equip us, enabling us to help others who may have gone through or are going through something similar and that was shown and revealed to us months later.

Clint had put up the Christmas tree and told me he had bumped an ornamental ashtray in the shape of a skull on our mantle. He then threw it away as that item had disturbed him and was not of the Lord. The Lord continued to show and reveal many things to us in our home over the next two years which we would need to get rid of – items with sun gods on them, certain antique dolls, types of jewellery pieces, many different new age books, an Eastern religious recipe book, evil eyes, dreamcatchers and healing crystals. Many of these items may have attachments to the occult and are also used in witchcraft. Things that we did not even know have attachments to the occult were shown to us.

The Holy Spirit guided us both as we cleansed and cleaned our home. We went on a family Christmas shopping spree at Gateway, all of us trying to get back to normal life as it used to be; only our lives would NEVER be the same, thanks to the powerful God we serve. He supernaturally changed us, He filled us with His Holy Spirit and He broke all our strongholds and bondages. We were like butterflies that had just gone through metamorphosis. We were sanctified and consecrated, radiating in His glory.

I went back to work and told people what had happened to us. Many did not believe us, saying we had had a breakdown – menopause – drugs – we heard it all. The truth is the devil tried to destroy us because he knew I had called out to God – BUT God is mighty to save!

Zephaniah 3:17
The Lord your God in your midst, The Mighty One, will save; He will rejoice over you with gladness, He will quiet you with His love, He will rejoice over you with singing.

All the demons in the world would not separate us from the love of God. It's difficult to come to terms with people not believing you, especially people you have known for years, who know your character and know that you don't lie and fabricate things. But God is our Comforter and our best Friend. He never leaves nor forsakes us especially during times of trouble. I realised that my strength was in Him and I could do all things through Him.

Philippians 4:13
I can do all things through Christ who strengthens me.

He was all we needed and, as Clint and I grew closer to God, so the two of us grew closer to each other. It does not worry me in the least who believes me or not. We know the truth – and so does God.

1) This present darkness
   Frank Peretti

2) A Celebration of Discipline
   Richard Foster.

   (Julian of Norwitch)

My prescription from the psychiatrist

My doctor's note

Patient: MR C MEJ Date: 29/11/2018
Address:
Age: Sex: [X] M [ ] F

The above pt was admitted in hospital with Acute Psychosis + Delusional state

MRi brain (N)
NFFD 26/11/18 – 30/11/18
He is under the care of
Dr. **CENSORED** (psychiatrist)

Clint's doctor's note

Chapter 6

Making the Commitment

My friend Penny, whom I have known for over thirty four years, told me about the movie *Faith like Potatoes*. I decided to buy Clint the DVD for Christmas as neither of us had read the book or seen the movie. About a week before Christmas, I retrieved a newspaper from our kitchen bin, not something I do on a regular basis. I opened it to an advert for a Shalom Ministries sermon to be held on 25th December 2018. I cut the advert out and stuck it on the fridge. I had no idea where Shalom Ministries was at the time. All I knew was that Angus Buchan was preaching there on 25th December 2018.

Clint came home that evening, immediately asking about the advert on the fridge. I told him I had no idea where Shalom was, but that if it was close by, perhaps we could attend. Clint looked it up on his cellphone and said it was in Greytown, a short drive from where we live in Pietermaritzburg. God has an amazing way of getting you to the right place at the right time. On that Christmas day in 2018, our family all landed up at Shalom listening to Uncle Angus give a powerful message on our Saviour, Jesus Christ. I recall Sharné fainting in the church that morning and something very special happened on the day we celebrated the birth of our King… we all committed our lives publicly to Jesus Christ – Clint, Sharné, Kelsey and myself. What a special moment. Thank You, Lord Jesus, for Your precious Blood that was shed for us on the Cross so we can spend eternity with You. Thank You for Your mercy and grace.

That night, we watched the movie *Faith like Potatoes,* a fitting end to a wonderful day.

God provides each of us with the Helper, the Holy Spirit, the Spirit of Truth *(Parakletos)* and He moved into our lives, into our hearts and into our souls. He transformed Clint and me completely. He flipped us like pancakes. We could NEVER have changed ourselves the way God changed us. We became new creations.

> **2 Corinthians 5:17**
> *Therefore, if anyone is in Christ, he is a new creation; old things have passed away; behold, all things have become new.*

I didn't understand what my brother and the Bible meant by being born again. Today, I fully understand what this means. It is through the Holy Spirit that we are born again into the kingdom of God. God renews our mind and restores our souls; the things of this world grow strangely dim and all you want is more of Him. You want to be in His presence all the time.

We both began to hunger and thirst for more of the Word and more of Jesus.

> **1 John 4:4**
> *You are of God, little children, and have overcome them, because He who is in you is greater than he who is in the world.*

Psalm 42:1
As the deer pants for the water brooks, So pants my soul for You, O God.

It's scary to look back and see where the devil had been leading us. Clint and I had spent my 40th birthday at *Teasers,* a strip club in Durban. We thought at the time it was fun, harmless and exciting, having a new adventure as a couple. We were also slowly but surely sucked into a world of endorsing and watching pornography, seeing it as healthy and positive for married couples, but not realising how addictive it was.

We used foul language frequently, with occasional binge drinking at friends parties, being the order of the day. We thought we were happy and 'living the life of Riley' but we were actually spiritually empty. It's amazing to see the power of God in our lives now and I truly pray that everyone reading this book will experience the true Presence of Jesus in their lives. Only He can break strongholds and change you from the inside out.

There is nothing better than developing a personal relationship with Jesus Christ and that is all He ever wants from us, to fellowship with us, but we get so caught up in the world that we become blinded to the truth. Now our spiritual eyes have opened and we see the incredible ways in which God speaks to us and the way He is moving in our lives.

Every day Clint and I start our day in prayer together and every evening we end our day together in prayer, thanking Jesus for everything He has done for us and for allowing us to experience the supernatural. We will never forget it and we will never turn our backs on Him.

We thank Him for dying on the Cross for our healing and restoration, for our salvation, protection, and provision. He is the Way Maker, the Miracle Worker, the Promise Keeper and the Light in the darkness. He is our Lord and Saviour – our God.

Luke 10:23-24
[23]Then He turned to His disciples and said privately, "Blessed are the eyes which see the things you see; [24]for I tell you that many prophets and kings have desired to see what you see, and have not seen it, and to hear what you hear, and have not heard it."

We repented of all our sins and God has forgiven us and, trust me, we had many. We are washed clean by His Blood which He shed for us on the Cross. We are now part of His family and we need to be the light to others. We need to pick up our cross and follow Him daily. It's not easy and we may fall and stumble along the way, but He is always there to pick us up.

Matthew 16:24
Then Jesus said to His disciples, "If anyone desires to come after Me, let him deny himself, and take up his cross, and follow Me…"

Matthew 5:14
You are the light of the world. A city that is set on a hill cannot be hidden.

Nowhere in the Bible does it say that the road will be easy. If anything, it will be harder because now our adversary, the devil, will try by all means necessary to keep us from inheriting the kingdom of Heaven. He has been there, seen its glory and beauty and he does not want you or me to go where he cannot go, where he was expelled from. But God has given us all the weaponry that we need to fight the good fight with and our faith continues to grow daily.

> **Deuteronomy 31:8**
> *And the LORD, He is the One who goes before you. He will be with you, He will not leave you nor forsake you; do not fear nor be dismayed.*

I pray that more people will seek Him. He is knocking at the door, waiting for you to open.

> **Revelation 3:20**
> *Behold, I stand at the door and knock. If anyone hears My voice and opens the door, I will come in to him and dine with him, and he with Me.*

> **Matthew 7:8**
> *For everyone who asks receives, and he who seeks finds, and to him who knocks it will be opened.*

Since our experience, God has spoken to us in so many ways and our faith grows daily. We have seen so many prayers answered. We have had revelations and confirmations. We serve a mighty King! Jesus is the one true God. He is so faithful and His promises are "yes and amen". Sometimes we don't understand everything but we realise that we now live by faith and not by sight and sometimes miracles take time. We put all our trust in the Lord.

> **Proverbs 3:5-6**
> *⁵Trust in the LORD with all your heart, and lean not on your own understanding; ⁶In all your ways acknowledge Him, and He shall direct your paths.*

Chapter 7

Walking in the Light

Clint and I were out shopping at Cascades Centre and, whilst in Clicks, he bumped into Guy, an old school friend. Guy immediately told Clint he looked different. He said Clint had a glow about him and Clint proceeded to inform him that he had recently given his life to the Lord. Guy was excited for him and said he would love to hear our testimony so, a few weeks later, we invited him around for dinner to share our testimony. Guy mentioned he was going to a church called *Revival Worship* and the pastor's name was Warren Schultz. Clint immediately knew whom he was referring to as a close friend of Clint's had recently mentioned that Warren would pray for people on the streets in Greytown many years ago. Guy told us how on fire Warren was for Jesus and he then invited Clint to join their Bible Study group.

I received a message from Debbie, an old friend of mine, requesting that I meet up with her. The last time I had seen her was at a drinking party at her house and things had not ended well. We had departed on bad terms. I thus declined and told her I held no grudges against her but felt we didn't need to meet up. Later that day, I received a message from my friend in the UK, Penny, informing me that Debbie was extremely ill. I felt terrible for declining her request to meet and immediately sent Debbie a message telling her I would like to meet with her. She refused, telling me not to bother, possibly due to being hurt from my initial decline. I told her I was sorry to hear that she was sick and said I would pray for her. I then sent her messages of encouragement and some Bible scriptures. Soon thereafter, it was Penny's birthday and I completely forgot to call and wish her. The following evening, when my oversight struck me, I called her. She told me she was shocked that I hadn't called her because I hadn't ever forgotten her birthday before. She then asked me if I had heard that Debbie was now in Greys Hospital in Pietermaritzburg. After the phone call, I told Clint we needed to visit Debbie immediately. When I saw her looking so sick and frail, it broke my heart. Clint and I stayed, chatting to her, until the security arrived, telling us we had to leave.

Two days later, Kelsey and I went to visit Debbie again. There were a lot of people visiting her at the time so I prayed for her and then we left. I had mentioned to Clint that I wanted Pastor Warren to pray with her. He said Warren had agreed to, as he had mentioned this to Warren at his Bible study group. Clint was going away the following day on a business trip so we agreed we would all go together the following evening. But God had other plans.

The next day, I was sitting at work when my sister, Linda, from Australia, called me to say she had heard from her mother-in-law that Debbie wasn't doing well. I immediately called Clint and told him. He said we should not wait until he returned but that I should call Pastor Warren and ask him to accompany me immediately to the hospital. I hadn't yet met Pastor Warren. I picked up the phone and dialled his number. I told him Debbie was very sick in hospital and I wasn't sure if she had committed her life to Jesus. I asked if he would be able to come with me that evening. He agreed and, after going quiet for a few seconds, being prompted by the Holy Spirit, he said, "Are you able to go now? I think we should go now". I said that would be fine and he agreed to fetch me from my workplace. We headed off to Greys Hospital. Our introduction was easy. It felt as if I had known him my whole life and the conversation just flowed. When we arrived at Greys, he prayed in the car for God to clear our path into the ward and make a way for us to enter, as Greys was very strict on visiting hours for non-family members. This visit was also outside of visiting hours.

He picked up his Bible and we managed to enter with no issues. Off we marched to Debbie's ward. When we arrived at her bedside, the first thing I noticed was that Debbie was wearing an oxygen mask and was unresponsive. I began to panic. I thought, 'God, how is she going to acknowledge You as her Lord and Saviour?' Odette, Debbie's mother, was standing at her bedside talking to a doctor. He left and, turning to me, she gave me a big hug. I hadn't seen her since my school days. The first thing she said to me was that Debbie had told her I had visited her and that she had seen such a change in me. She had told her mom that I was different, to which her mom had replied that she could also have that change and that only Jesus could do that.

I introduced Pastor Warren to Odette. We all knelt at her bedside and began to pray. Pastor Warren prayed fervently and took Debbie's hand, asking her to squeeze his, should she wish to commit her life to Jesus. We watched and there was no movement at all. Debbie was motionless. Odette cried out for Debbie to squeeze Warren's hand, frantically wanting Debbie to recommit her life to the Lord. She had said that Debbie was in a backslidden state. Pastor Warren told her to remain calm and continued to pray fervently. He gently placed his hand on Debbie's head, continuing to hold her hand and pray. He then asked her to squeeze his hand if she acknowledged the Lord Jesus Christ as her own personal Lord and Saviour. We watched with baited breath as Debbie squeezed Pastor Warren's hand. She took in a deep, gasping breath. We all got such a fright. Debbie acknowledged that Jesus was the Son of God and that He had died and rose again. Debbie was saved, as the Bible tells us in *Romans 10:9*. Pastor Warren, Odette and I marvelled and tears of sheer joy streamed down our cheeks. That was the last movement she made and, soon thereafter, she passed away as the Lord received her to Himself. The Psalm that the Lord gave me that day was *Psalm 65* which mentions salvation.

That was the beginning of my walk with Pastor Warren, a God-fearing man who has stood by my family's side ever since and has taught us so much. He was radically transformed from being an ex-Club bouncer to a humble servant of Jesus Christ, unselfishly giving of his time to serve others.

Jesus moved into our lives and into our home. It was laid on our hearts to put up a scripture on the wall of our home – Joshua 24:15 *"...as for me and my house, we will serve the Lord."* Clint and I discussed it. However, we were unsure if I should paint it on a wooden frame, paint it directly onto the wall or if we should have a sticker made. Clint went for his daily run and I told him to pray about it. He returned later that morning and handed me a small piece of clear paper. I peeled it. It was a sticker he had found in his path whilst jogging and our decision was made. Amazingly, I was put into contact with a lady who manufactured stickers. It turned out that we were both at school together and she was now fellowshipping at *One Life Church*. She made a beautiful sticker for us and spent time explaining how to put it on the wall. We love that sticker and it's a statement we've made publicly for all to see.

Thereafter, we wanted to put up a cross in our front garden as a symbol of whom we serve. God's Hand was in the project from the start. We were put in contact with a gentleman who sold old railway sleepers and we went to his business to look at the stock he had on hand. We met one of his staff members who showed us the sleepers. There were loads of heavy, chunky sleepers set aside and we knew we would have to cut one of them to size in order for the cross to be perfectly balanced. We hadn't yet made a final decision and returned the following day when we met the owner. He said we needed to choose the sleepers we wanted, whereafter he would put them aside for collection. We moved loads of sleepers until we were happy with our choice of two. We then noticed one sleeper which was smaller than all the rest. It was also the only one that was different and it was the perfect measurement. To us, that was a miracle.

There would be no cutting required and it would make the cross so much neater. We could hardly believe it. Our friend, Kyle, who owns a bakkie, kindly offered to assist us with collecting the sleepers. We discovered that the owner of the business was a follower of Christ who put Clint on his daily devotional WhatsApp group. The metal sheeting, which was required to secure the cross at the base, was also acquired miraculously with the perfect thickness and height. God is amazing! He provided exactly what was required for this project. Duane agreed to erect the cross and spent hours assembling it. We put lights all around it and it automatically switches on as the sun sets. What a beautiful cross he made. It reminds us daily of the sacrifice Jesus made for each and every single one of us – He loved us that much!

The Cross we erected in our garden as a proclamation of who we serve

Chapter 8

A Humbling Experience

22 January 2019 – Tuesday

My mom suffered a heart attack and a mild stroke early on this Tuesday morning. Doctors were surprised that she had both at the same time as this is very uncommon. I thank the Lord for the window cleaner, Bongiwe, who heard my mom's cries as she was cleaning the house next door, a miracle quite frankly. Mom tried pressing the remote panic button which was around her neck. It was not working! The windows in my mom's house were all closed. Bongiwe heard her as she lay on the floor shouting for help. She called the security office who in turn called me.

Clint and I took my mom to Howick Mediclinic where the doctor told us she was in heart failure. My spiritual warfare during November was now happening and playing out in front of my eyes – the feeling that my mother, who was unsaved at the age of 84, was going to die. I had seen a number plate with '85' and my mom's birthday was only in April so I had to put all my trust in the Lord and leave her in His hands. He was in control. I wasn't going to allow any of the lies of the devil to plague my mind. I had the full armour of God on.

I had on the belt of truth, the breastplate of righteousness, my feet prepared with the gospel of peace, the shield of faith, the helmet of salvation, and the Sword of the Spirit.

Ephesians 6:10-11
[10]Finally, my brethren, be strong in the Lord and in the power of His might. [11]Put on the whole armor of God, that you may be able to stand against the wiles of the devil.

My mom was still an atheist and wanted nothing to do with pastors at this stage. She was telling us to stay clear of them, telling us they are bad people and mostly con artists. BUT GOD. He has such a sense of humour and ensured that my mom was surrounded by pastors over the next few weeks. The father of the lady in her ward was a pastor from the same area where my mom grew up, in England, and they chatted for some time as they had so much in common. They reminisced about the old days in the UK. Even her roommates at the step-down facility at Wembley House were Christians, reading their Bibles, and had pastors visiting them from time to time and praying. My mom couldn't wait to tell us this. Clint and I constantly planted seeds and prayed for her and with her. It was wonderful to see how she accepted prayer and allowed us to pray with her.

Some key dates of various incidents that took place

17 February 2019 – Sunday

Clint and I drove my mom back to Howick on this warm Sunday morning. She was not quite ready to go back to her own home yet, still being rather frail but doing remarkably well. We booked her into the Amber Valley respite stepdown section. Clint and I both smiled when she said "Pastors aren't all that bad" on our drive up. It was evident to us how God was working in her life in an incredible way.

Driving from the recovery home in Pietermaritzburg to the care centre in Howick, we saw a kaleidoscope of butterflies that we all commented on as we found it quite amazing. The highway seemed littered with thick clusters of butterflies, all different sizes and colours. We stopped at the Howick Pharmacy to collect medicine which had been prescribed for my mom and were greeted with an amazing show by a dragonfly in front of our car's windscreen. I recall Clint asking my mom if she liked dragonflies and she told him it was her favourite insect growing up as a child.

When we arrived at her room at the care centre in Howick we were amazed to see her bedroom décor duvet cover. It was full of butterflies, dragonflies and ladybirds. Clint peeked into the other rooms to see if they were all decorated the same but they were not. We prayed with my mom and then left. We had seen butterflies and a dragonfly and, only when we were approaching our car, did we see the beautiful red ladybird fly into the car as it came to rest on the dashboard. Both Clint's and my jaw dropped and we just knew God's Hand was in this.

We giggled the whole way home thinking about how God had changed my mom's mind about pastors and how the room's décor was just so fitting for the day we had just witnessed. God was working and moving in my mom's life. Prayers were being answered. I am always so amazed at how God works all things for the good of those who love Him. We were amazed at the miracle show we had received on this day and, more than two years later, Clint and I are still so amazed at His goodness and we are often in awe of how He works.

Mark 9:23
"All things are possible to him who believes..."

28 June 2019 – Friday

My 85-year-old mom went through her own spiritual warfare which lasted exactly 40 hours. She wrote all about it in her personal diary. At 3 pm on the 28th June, my mom had lost movement in her legs and fell off the toilet. She said she lost hours and only regained consciousness at 3 am. She lay there waiting for some sort of feeling to come back, but it didn't. She was unable to get up, so she had to pull herself around on the floor. The most obvious thing to have done would have been to press the emergency button which she carried around her neck. This would have alerted security and they would have attended to her immediately.

However, when we asked her why she hadn't just pressed the button, she said that a voice in her head would not allow her to push the panic button. She lay on the cold floor in the middle of winter for two nights, not even being able to switch on any lights or to drink or eat anything. I can't even begin to put myself in that situation and I can't even imagine what she must have gone through. All I can say is that the sight of my mom, when I finally saw her, would have brought tears to anyone's eyes. She told us it was spiritual warfare. The devil tried to kill my mom and was playing with her mind, inner voices constantly telling her not to push the button. Finally, at 7 am on Sunday, 30th June, she humbled herself and cried out to God for help and then only was she finally able to push the panic button around her neck.

The clinic nurse called to alert me about what had happened. Clint, Kelsey and I rushed up to Howick. My mom was already in the ambulance when we reached her house and the paramedic told me not to go in as I would be shocked at the state of it. Kelsey went with my mom in the ambulance and we followed behind. We were listening to the song called *New Wine* on our way to the hospital. When we saw my mom, she had tears streaming down her face and the first thing she said to us was that she felt like a squashed grape. I immediately thought of the song we had just been listening to in our car and I then played it for her.

Here are some of the lyrics:

In the crushing
In the pressing
You are making new wine
In the soil
I now surrender
You are breaking new ground

So I yield to You into Your careful hand
When I trust You I don't need to understand

Make me Your vessel
Make me an offering
Make me whatever You want me to be
I came here with nothing
But all You have given me
Jesus bring new wine out of me

Jesus allowed my mom to be crushed like a grape so that she would be able to bring forth new wine.

Sometimes we have issues such as pride and unforgiveness that need to be dealt with and God will ensure that He humbles us where and when necessary. He was ultimately in control.

Our hearts broke seeing her so frail and fragile with her

body battered, bruised and full of raw sores from dragging herself on the carpets over the 40-hour period. Yet she was so strong, surviving two nights in the middle of winter on the cold floor. When you start drawing closer to God, the enemy attacks. When you are walking in darkness, he leaves you alone.

Clint said my mom's Psalm was *Psalm 23* and he read it to her that morning. On 30th June 2019, we had the privilege of leading my mother to Christ. We prayed the sinner's prayer with her and she confessed Jesus Christ as her Lord and Saviour.

> **Romans 10:9**
> *that if you confess with your mouth the Lord Jesus and believe in your heart that God has raised Him from the dead, you will be saved.*

She had to work out her salvation with fear and trembling.

> **Philippians 2:12**
> *Therefore, my beloved, as you have always obeyed, not as in my presence only, but now much more in my absence, work out your own salvation with fear and trembling.*

That was one of my happiest days and proudest moments of my life, a moment that Clint and I will never forget. My 85-year-old mother was saved and truly saved this time.

Over the next few months, we were privileged to pray with her and every day I would read her scriptures. Nourishing our souls with the living Word of God is critical and a very important, vital part of our journey with our living God. God opened a door for her and, no matter what the devil threw her way, God's warring angels never left her side, protecting her against all the schemes of the evil one. She moved into a place just down the road from our house which made popping in for a daily visit and scripture reading so easy and convenient.

The care home had just opened but she was not happy there, saying that she sensed an evil presence in that house. A few days later, my mom had a terrible fall as the night nurses were putting her to bed. They pushed the bed and my mom went flying forward, face first, cutting open her forehead. Watching the CCTV footage from her bedroom, which had just been installed a few days prior, was extremely traumatic and brought tears to my eyes. She was rushed to the hospital for stitches.

My mom also had a supernatural encounter with the Holy Spirit after my cousin, Lisa, had prayed fervently for her that same morning to have an encounter with the Holy Spirit. My mom cried when she told me her experience. She said that when she spoke to the other lady in the house, she knew it was not her speaking and that it was an amazing experience. Shortly after that, we moved my mom to *Riverside Care Centre*. On her first day there, the cupboard pelmet fell on her head. The staff there said it had never happened before. Again, my mom cried as she told me that God kept on saving her. That fall and the hit to her head could have killed her, but God was not done yet.

He had a perfect plan still laid out and was still softening my mom's heart. We watched her grow spiritually and she eventually became a prayer warrior. She went from hating music to saying how beautifully the choir at *Riverside Home* sang and, on 10th November 2019, she went to her first church service in over 60 years. Pastor Keith gave a sermon on lepers, a subject close to her heart as she spent many years working at the leper colony at Mkambati. She even wrote in her diary that it touched a soft spot. God is AMAZING!!!

The Lord came for my mom on the 1st December 2019 whilst Clint and I were in Israel. We were not at her bedside when God took her home but the Holy Spirit lead me to give my mom a call and to talk and pray with her. It was the last day of our trip and we were waiting at the airport for our flight home. I told Clint I was going for a walk and I called Sharné. I asked her to put the phone to my mom's ear so I could speak to her and pray with her. Even though she was on life support and unconscious, her blood pressure machine went crazy as I prayed with her. It went from 40 to 100 and I knew right there and then that she had heard me.

I knew God had given me that moment to say goodbye. Others said she was in a coma and could not hear me because she had already basically died two days earlier but that is just not true. She heard me alright. Kelsey and Colin, who were at her bedside at the time I called, confirmed that they had seen and heard her machine go crazy while I spoke to her and that it had not happened before, nor did it happen again afterwards. I thank the Lord for providing me with that moment of closure.

Amazingly enough, Clint found me at the airport wondering around just as I was about to say goodbye and I then handed the phone to him so he could also speak to my mom. That then started a chain reaction until everybody in the family was able to say goodbye and then the Lord came for her soon afterwards.

A lady in the bathroom at the airport's departure terminal approached me and put her arms around me. She told me that Jesus wanted me to know that He loved me. I couldn't stop crying and I was deeply touched by her message.

When Clint and I finally stood in the boarding queue, this young girl, whom Uncle Angus had prayed for a few days earlier, came up to me and frantically wanted to show me what was on her parent's phone. I apologised to the parents as the little girl pushed and shoved her way over the people to ensure that I could see the photo on the phone. I was surprised to see that it was a picture of something I had also taken – a photo at *Mensa Christi* on the sea of Galilee, the place where Jesus had appeared to His disciples after His crucifixion when He cooked them breakfast on the shore.

They were zooming into the picture to see the cross on the water. I had also noticed that in the picture I had taken and had zoomed into it to show Clint. The reason I had taken the photo was because we had all been standing in the hot sun, waiting to be anointed by Uncle Angus. His daughter had then prayed for some shade covering and then this beautiful cloud covered the sun. As I looked down at the lady's phone, I just knew God was saying, *"I have your mom"*.

Her favourite number was 13 and Luke 13:13 says, *"And He laid His hands on her, and immediately she was made straight, and glorified God."*

My mom now has eternity through His grace. I think of her often and miss her terribly but I know I will see her again one day in our Father's house.

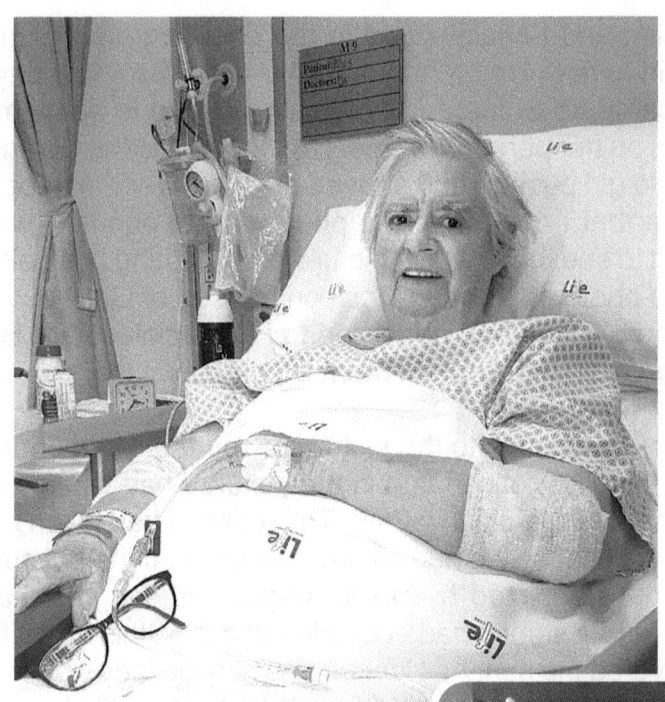

My Mom shortly after her recovery in hospital, committed her life to the Lord

Mom with the panic button she always carried around her neck

The cloud photograph taken at Mensa Christi

Chapter 9

A Trip to the Holy Land

The way we got to Israel was a miracle. Clint had heard there was a tour, an It's Time tour with Angus Buchan and he said that we should go. I told him we didn't even know our Bible that well and we should wait awhile, but God had other plans and, after God gave Clint a distinct sign and confirmation 'strike while the iron is hot', one thing led to another and, before we knew it, Clint had booked the trip.

We were unsure how we were even going to pay for it. Amazingly, a surprise amount equivalent to the value of the trip was deposited into Clint's bank account a week prior to having to make full payment. God is amazing.

Family and friends had criticised Angus Buchan, saying he was a chauvinist, a false teacher and a con artist. We heard it all. Funny how not one of them had ever even met the man, Angus Buchan.

Honestly, I can say that in all the encounters that we have had with Uncle Angus, and there have been many, he has been nothing but kind, loving and respectable, an absolute gentleman, a true man of God. I haven't met anyone who has such a love for people as he does and who gives so much of his time to do God's work.

This was so evident on our tour in Israel. He always ensured that he spoke to everyone and anointed everyone. I even recall the one night, after our *It's Time* prayer meeting, it was cold and late but Uncle Angus insisted that he hug and say goodbye to each and every person who had attended that meeting – well over 250 people. I remember looking at Clint in disbelief and amazement and we both thought about how Uncle Angus really loves what he does. Most people would rather just rush off to their warm, cozy hotel rooms.

Even on our plane ride home, he came and spoke to each one of us individually, being concerned for our wellbeing as our plane had dropped a few meters mysteriously and many passengers had been injured through this incident. But God had us all in the palm of His Hand.

The trip was absolutely perfect, from seeing all the wonderful places where Jesus taught, where He walked, where He performed many of His miracles, where He was crucified, to sailing on the Sea of Galilee, singing *Bless the Lord, O my soul*. A magnificent pink cloud in the shape of a cross, appearing above us in the sky, was a sight none of us will ever forget.

> **Acts 2:19**
> *I will show wonders in heaven above And signs in the earth beneath: Blood and fire and vapor of smoke.*

We witnessed healing miracles and met the most amazing people, brothers and sisters in Christ, with whom we keep in contact to this day. We were baptised by Uncle Angus in the Jordan River on 29th November 2019. Our old self had died and a new creation was made.

Romans 6:6
knowing this, that our old man was crucified with Him, that the body of sin might be done away with, that we should no longer be slaves of sin.

I was amazed at how God was moving in our lives. I had thought about calling our Pastor, Warren, and requesting him to pray with my mom whilst in hospital and, truth be told, I was praying he would bump into my sister at the hospital as well. I hadn't asked him to go because I knew he was busy and had a lot on his plate. After church that Sunday, the Holy Spirit led him to go to the hospital and pray with my mom and he did bump into my sister as well.

Leaving *En Gedi* on the last day of our trip, we sat on the bus and noticed Warren had sent Clint a voice note. Clint put one earpiece in his ear and I put the other one in mine. We listened to Warren's message about how he had gone to the hospital earlier that day and prayed with my mom. He had bumped into my sister. My jaw dropped as he relayed the story.

We drove to the airport and it was the first time on our entire trip that the people on the bus starting singing. We began with the song *Way Maker*. Noel, an Australian friend whom we had met on tour, prayed with Clint and me for my mom. Our prayers were heard and that is why today I believe the Holy Spirit led me to call my mom from the airport so I could have my final goodbye.

One of the ladies I had the privilege of meeting on our tour was *Jenny Blume*. Here is her testimony in her own words:

Pool of Bethesda –
The day the Lord healed my eyes

Since I was a little girl, I had problems with my eyes. The Ophthalmologist diagnosed it with the longest name, a name that I cannot even pronounce. Basically, it meant that I had to use antibiotic eyedrops for the rest of my life until I became a grey-haired old lady. Being so young, I didn't really understand what it all meant, but complete lifestyle changes needed to be made. I had to change my diet and I had to wear specially made sunglasses all the time.

I remember whenever the seasons would change my eyes would become so red and irritated that it literally felt like I wanted to scratch my eyes out. And every single person would ask me, "Why are your eyes so red?" When I was young it didn't bother me that much, but when I became older, the questions got worse. People thought that I was on drugs. Asking me if I'm an alcoholic. Do I get enough sleep? The comments and questions were so relentless and I became so self-conscious about it. I never wanted to look someone straight in the eye, which made me seem so rude, but it was because I didn't want them to comment or question the redness of my eyes. One would think that the eyedrops would at least help, but they didn't really and financially it was tough. Every six months I had go for doctors' appointments, always wishing that it would finally be the last or at least that there would be some sort of improvement.

Throughout my childhood, I would pray and ask the Lord to heal my eyes but, at some point, I stopped praying. I stopped asking because it didn't seem like my prayers were being heard. I mean, there are so many things happening in this world, why would the Lord even bother to listen to my (what I thought were) insignificant prayers. He had bigger prayers to answer. The Lord asked me this question one day that really rocked me to my core and I had to think about it, like really think about it, because the question was a tough one to answer. The Lord asked me, *"Jenny, if I never heal your eyes this side of Heaven, would you still serve Me the way you serve Me now?"* That was all He needed to ask me. It took me days, months actually, of fighting and praying to finally come to the answer to say, *"Yes, Lord. If this is Your Will not to heal me this side of Heaven, then I will accept that."* And there was a supernatural peace that came over me when I prayed those words. It was truly amazing.

Another miracle was that the Lord blessed me with a trip to Israel in 2019. He provided financially for the trip enabling me to go. I did not have to spend one penny. It was all in His marvelous plan on what would happen to me while I was there. What He would do.

The whole Israel trip was amazing. I was baptised in the Jordan River where Jesus Christ was baptised – I was truly humbled by that. It was amazing to see and experience where Jesus Christ walked and did His miracles. To see where He was crucified.

It was on one of the last few days that we went to the Pool of Bethesda – where in Bible times an angel would stir the water and whoever jumped into the water first would be healed from every sickness/disease. So that afternoon, Uncle Angus Buchan prayed for me. He didn't know what he was praying for but I knew and God knew. I had faith that my eyes would be healed.

And, as I am writing this on Tuesday, 4th May 2021, I have never had to put in one single eyedrop into my eyes. My eyes don't itch anymore. My eyes were healed!! All the Glory and Honour and Praise goes to the King of kings – God Almighty!

Everyone's journey with the Lord is different and His ways are not our ways. Sometimes He doesn't heal someone and sometimes He does. He has His reasons and purposes for everything He does. We have to come to that place to be able to say "Not my will, but Your will be done, Lord". That is when true freedom comes. That is when the Lord can work in your life because you've given it over to Him.

I hope my testimony helps at least one person. To God be the Glory and Honour and Praise, forever and ever. Amen!

by Jenny Blume

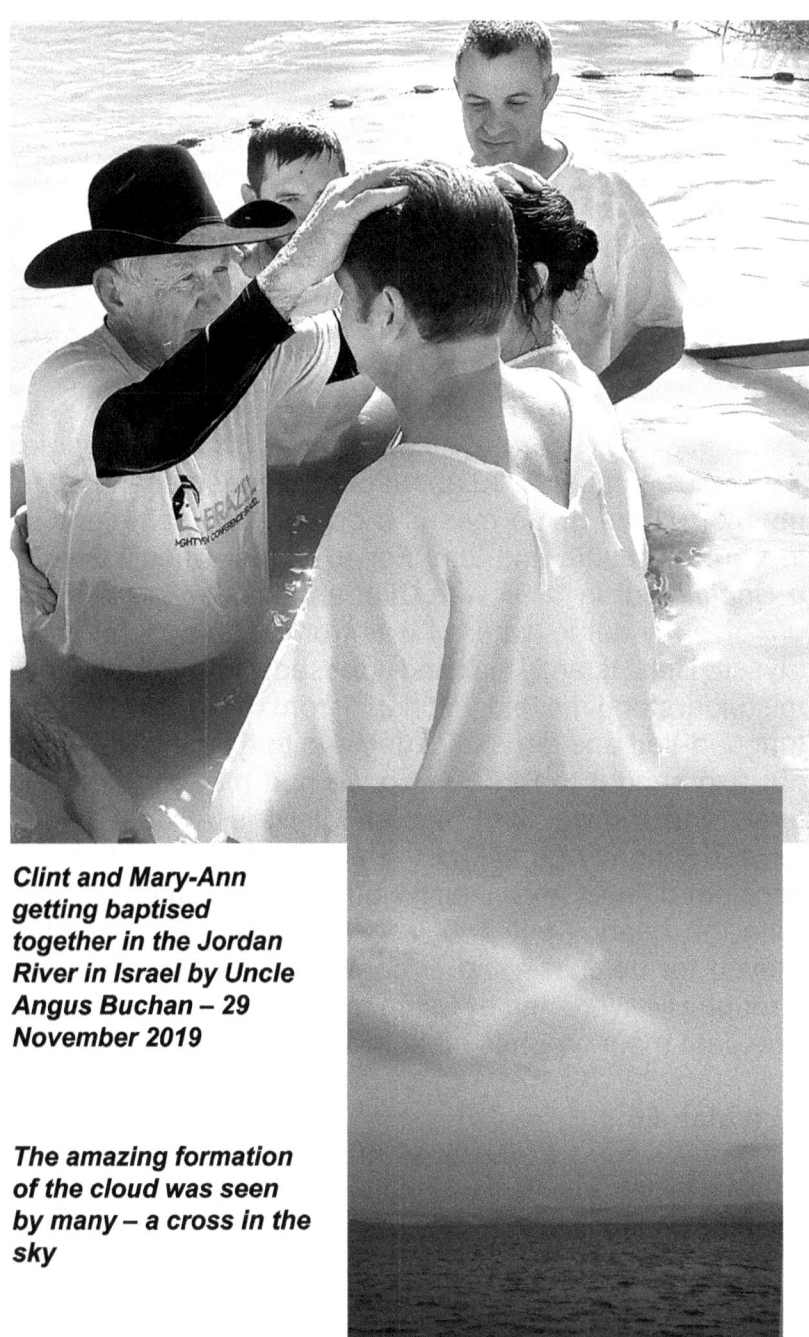

Clint and Mary-Ann getting baptised together in the Jordan River in Israel by Uncle Angus Buchan – 29 November 2019

The amazing formation of the cloud was seen by many – a cross in the sky

Chapter 10

～ Testimonies ～

I was asked to share my testimony at Shalom Ministries on 8th December 2019 about our trip to Israel and about my mom. I am by no means a person who can stand up in front of people and talk. For example, when I was on a *Contiki* tour in 1994 with Clint and was asked to stand up, give my name, where I was from and say a bit about myself, I felt instantly sick and stressed. I love talking, don't misunderstand me, but just not in front of big crowds. I get tongued-tied and nervous. I decided to type my testimony out and send it to Ronel, who we had met on the trip to Israel and she works at Shalom Ministries. Ronel agreed to read it on my behalf, but she said that I should really consider doing it myself as it would be more impactful and from the heart. I put it to God and prayed hard on it. I prayed for boldness and strength and God spoke to me through His Word and by using my cousin with a scripture. She sent me a prophesy that morning –

Isaiah 66:9
"Shall I bring to the time of birth, and not cause delivery?" says the Lord. "Shall I who cause delivery shut up the womb?" says your God.

When I looked at my Bible, open on my dining room table, it was open on that exact page. I just knew God was telling me to step up to the plate, step out of my comfort zone and to be bold and courageous, trusting in the Lord. When we arrived at Shalom on that Sunday morning, I went to the bathroom and, behind the door, I read Joshua 1:9: *"Have I not commanded you? Be strong and of good courage; do not be afraid, nor be dismayed, for the Lord your God is with you wherever you go."*

God was with me that morning and the testimony went well – all glory to God.

During the first year or so, after committing our lives to Christ, it felt as though God was talking to us all the time. We could hardly believe how He was shaping us and speaking to us in so many different ways. Clint and I were literally blown away daily at His presence felt in our lives and, as soon as we arrived home from work, we couldn't wait to convey our stories for the day to each other, practically talking over each other in the excitement. I would call my sister in Australia and my friend, Penny, in the UK daily with stories of miracles and how God was moving in our lives. Then slowly the incidents seemed to be happening less and less and my brother explained it to me so nicely because he knew exactly what he was talking about as he had experienced the same thing.

When we give our lives to Christ, we are like new babies, new creations which He needs to nurture and feed. Then He puts us onto solid food and, as we learn and grow in His Word, we need to start walking by faith and not by sight.

2 Corinthians 5:7
For we walk by faith, not by sight.

His Word promises that He sticks closer to us than a brother. He continues to protect and watch over us and

He continues to speak to us through His Word. It is very clear that in order to build our faith we need to read our Bibles.

> **Romans 10:17**
> *So then faith comes by hearing, and hearing by the word of God.*

My sister, Linda, and I have grown in the Lord in leaps and bounds. She told me she always thought she was a Christian but, only after witnessing what happened to us, did she truly then build a relationship with our Lord Jesus Christ and she became a reborn Christian. We have both spent hours and hours talking about the Lord and, even though we are miles apart, we are closer than ever. I love you, my beautiful sister in Christ and I thank you for all your love and support.

My friend, Penny, also told me that, through what had happened to Clint and me, she is now reading her Bible much more and has also grown in leaps and bounds. We also spend hours talking about our Lord and Saviour. I am truly thankful for our friendship.

It took me over 30 years to finally ask my brother to share his testimony with us. I suppose all those years earlier I wasn't interested in hearing anything about God and, quite frankly, at the mention of the Name of Jesus, I would feel very uncomfortable. Now, as new Christians, we were excited and eager to hear it. We sat in their lounge as we listened intently while he relayed his story, often bringing tears to his eyes and ours.

Here is his testimony, in his own words:

My nickname in the army was 'Mad Moffett'. I was an angry, wild and frustrated young man. Most weekends I would end up in the gutter – too drunk to even remember how I got there. My language was foul and I was a womaniser. I volunteered to attend an army camp as I did not know what direction my life was taking. At the camp I met a couple of guys who befriended me and invited me to stay with their family in Ballito for the weekend. They went to church on the Sunday and invited me to go with them. I declined and went for a walk on the beach instead. The next weekend, they invited me to Ballito again. Again, on the Sunday morning, they invited me to church and again I declined.

I was still in bed when I heard an audible voice saying to me, "Moffett, you are a real coward. You cannot even go to church!" I had been in active service in the army and no-one was going to call me a coward! I leapt out of bed, grabbed a T-shirt and rushed after them – leaving the house in my sleeping shorts, having not brushed my hair or cleaned my teeth. I cannot remember the church service as nothing untoward happened there.

Afterwards we went for lunch with some people from the church and a woman came up to me and said God had told her to pray for me. I vehemently turned down her offer and told her I did not need any prayer. She persisted and I told her that if God showed Himself to me like He had showed Himself to all of them then I would also believe. She did not pursue the matter any further. As we were about to leave to drive back to the army camp, the group huddled in the lounge to pray for our safe travels. As I bowed my head, wishing they would hurry up, I felt a supernatural hand upon my back pushing me to the middle of the room and onto my knees. I resisted but the force was too great and eventually I feel onto my knees – my pride broke and I wept like I have never wept before. The experience is hard to describe but I can only say that it was like fire that was moving through my whole body. I was being wrung out like a sopping wet towel before the powerful Hand of God. The group couldn't believe what was happening. They all stopped praying and stared at me, but I was unaware of anything apart from the mighty presence of God. When eventually I was helped to my feet, totally spent, I felt like an entirely new creation, which I can only equate to the smell you get when you open a brand-new car with leather seats. I had been turned completely inside out.

During the course of the next week, I continued to weep as I came to comprehend the magnitude of what God had done for me. The stronghold of swearing, womanising and alcohol were broken. I literally was a new creation, washed clean by the Blood of Jesus Christ. As I submitted my life to the will of God, the miracles continued which included being accepted into varsity to study architecture – this for someone who had not even passed matric maths! At varsity, my nickname was 'Moffett the Prophet' – what a change from 'Mad Moffett'!

by David Moffett

I am so proud of my brother and I am so thankful for all the years that he covered my family and myself in prayer. He is my brother in Christ. I love you, David. Thank you for sharing your testimony.

I would love to share some amazing encounters with you. We have been on this incredible journey with God. We have experienced His unfailing love and His presence in our lives and seen His Hand at work in those around us. We have met the most incredible God-fearing people – brothers and sisters in Christ – and have been able to share in the joy of the gospel. God has placed people in our lives whom we were able to assist because of what we had experienced and gone through, which has been an absolute privilege. All glory to the Lord! We say, "Use us, please, Lord, use us".

On our return trip from Israel, Clint was asked to do a presentation of our trip at *Revival Worship.* I was in London with Kelsey at the time as she was starting an *au pair* job. Mother hen wanted to ensure all was in order there before leaving her baby chick behind even though I know I put all my trust in the Lord Jesus Christ. Clint had decided to just give a brief rundown of our spiritual warfare before doing his presentation of Israel. That is when a gentleman, who hadn't been to the church before, heard about the warfare and later approached Clint to ask if he could please come and talk to us about what he had experienced over the last few months.

A few weeks later, we were sitting in our lounge listening to him relay his story about what had been happening to him and his ex-girlfriend at her house after they had started getting involved with crystals. Nothing could shock us and we believed every word he said. We could relate to a lot of it. He had even said his ex-girlfriend had called her dad satan, something that Clint had also done. A lot of what they had experienced was terrifying and they could not understand what was going on at the time. He said his ex-girlfriend wanted nothing to do with him as she felt he was the cause of all the problems and she believed he was evil and wanted to kill her – exactly how I had felt about Clint. The devil was using similar tactics to deceive them.

They had both recommitted their lives to God but it took prayer and fasting for the ex-girlfriend to fully understand what had happened to them and to finally send him a message as we completed the third day of our fast. She told him the war was not with flesh and blood but was with the unseen realm. Thank You, Jesus, for Your faithfulness and hearing our prayers and petitions.

This is her testimony in her own words:

I believe in miracles because I am one. The only reason I am alive today is because of God's grace and His love for me. I was saved and baptised when I was young, but I did not understand the true meaning of this. My sin started a long time ago when I was trying to find love and acceptance and belonging from the world – a place I never belonged. I never knew God on a personal level or the depth of His love for me. I made the wrong decisions and made wrong friends and I lived a sinful life. This all led me down a long road of pain and disappointment – a slow death sentence. For the past 17 years I have been partying, drinking and using drugs, in and out of failed relationships and wondering why I was still so empty inside and I felt so alone.

This lifestyle of mine ended me up into rehabs, seeing psychologists, psychiatrists and, in the end, none of it helped. It just made me feel more worthless and sent me into deeper depression – I was lost. Death became a welcoming friend, an option less painful than the life I was living. This being said, I would rather want to focus on our Father's amazing grace and how far it reaches and what lengths He is willing to go for us. Every bad decision I ever made for whatever selfish reason I had at the time is exactly where I needed to be. While I was chasing something I never understood, while running away from the drama and chaos I was creating, I was getting closer to breaking point. I was getting closer to God and He was patiently waiting for me. He was waiting for me to surrender and to admit I could not carry on, on my own. I needed Him.

Transferring to Camperdown in 2017 was not a coincidence. I believe it was in His plan. A colleague at work would always speak about Jesus and how good He was. She would always chat to me about Him and encourage me to pray. God puts people in our lives to help us find Him. I believe that. Things got a lot worse before they got better and this was my own fault. I started dabbling in crystals, chakras and looking into different beliefs and religions instead of looking to Jesus. This is where life got very dark and very scary. Strange unexplainable things were happening. I won't discuss this as I am not equipped at this point to try and explain or understand what was going on. I do, however, understand it as spiritual warfare. I just knew that I couldn't continue down the path and I needed help. I needed Him.

This was a very strange and confusing time in my

life. What I experienced and felt is very difficult to explain. The day of my deliverance was Monday 13 January 2020. I hadn't slept for three days straight. I was an absolute wreck and I was frightened. How I managed to get to Camperdown that morning, only God knows. All I wanted was my freedom and I wanted freedom from the hell that I was suffering. I told this friend of mine at work that I needed help. I felt like I was on the verge of dying. I felt like my whole body was shaking and vibrating from the inside out. She put me in the vehicle and she took me to her sister's house. She was so calm amongst my chaos. I am not too sure when it hit me but there was this sudden panic and realisation that I couldn't trust what was happening around me. I was afraid for my life. I truly thought I was going to die and the craziest thing entered my head. They were going to kill me. This of course was far from the truth. At the time, I think it was that which was inside of me that was afraid because it knew that its time was up. It was coming to an end.

When we arrived at Pastor Sibisi's house, everything happened so fast. It was a blur of the memory and I can't recall all the details. I remember refusing to leave the car because I was too afraid, but eventually I made it inside. I remember people were praying in the background while Mama Sibisi was trying to talk to me. I remember thinking that this was all a mistake and that it was crazy. These people were crazy. I needed to get out of there. The storm inside of me was raging and there was so much chaos going on within myself. I can't remember how we ended up sitting on the floor but there we were.

The last thing I remember was a sudden calmness

inside of me, after feeling like I was losing my mind and running in a million directions all at once. I was suddenly so calm and at peace, like it was all a bad dream. I knew it wasn't though. I remember looking into Mama's eyes, not her own eyes though – they were different. They were brighter. They were like a golden amber, a honey colour. They were so beautiful and I will never forget them. I still believe that these were the eyes of my Saviour, Jesus Christ. He delivered me that day by this anointed person. He rescued me from death and that day was the start of my life. I could feel I was different. I could feel I was lighter inside. I was free. Since that day, I have not craved a cigarette, I haven't craved alcohol, I haven't used drugs and I don't want to. Whatever demons were plaguing me for so long were no longer there. I was healed. My one true love, Jesus Christ, saved me from myself. I have finally found what I had been desperately searching for most of my life. I have found home. I am never looking back.

by Katherine Buller

A few months later, the Lord brought someone else across our path. We had invited our worship leader, Marius, and his wife, Surette, for dinner and we began chatting about our personal testimony. Marius then mentioned a phone call he had received from his dad the previous night. His dad was very concerned about a lady in his church who was experiencing very strange and unexplainable things. His dad was trying to look up information on spiritual warfare on the internet as he hadn't really dealt with this sort of thing before and the lady was desperate for help.

He was away at the time and had called his son for advice. We were asked if we would be happy to meet with her. Clint and I of course agreed and the next day we met with her. Most people would think she had gone totally mad, by listening to her speaking about people following her, watching her, torturing and tormenting her. But we listened and understood because of what we had experienced ourselves.

She was experiencing demonic activity in her life. Scary and terrible things were happening to her. We soon realised that a door had been opened when her housemate had decided to go to a witchdoctor for advice on some stolen items, not realising that, by doing this, he was inviting demons into his life and into the home where they stayed. She had confessed that, as a young lady, she had often visited a clairvoyant for counsel and advice. This too opened the door and gave the enemy legal rights to wreak havoc in her life.

A few nights later, she was back in our home as a few of us gathered around to offer prayer and support. We also had a lady by the name of René whom the Lord had put in our lives. She was equipped in deliverance ministry and she immediately identified that the lady sitting in our lounge (Hannelie) had unforgiveness in her heart. She opened up to us about harbouring unforgiveness in her heart for a childhood boyfriend who had broken her heart in high school. She forgave him and recommitted her life to Jesus that night.

The Lord worked in her and put the right people in her path and she was delivered from her demons. We remain friends to this day.

Here is her testimony in her own words:

It's March 2020 and the start of lockdown. With the extra time at hand, I tried a few new recipes and brushed up on my cooking skills. One evening, I was deep-frying potatoes when hot oil started splashing wildly so I tried to move the pot and, in the process, I dropped it and that caused second-degree burns on my foot.

Soon after this incident, strange events started to take place. It felt like all my surrounding neighbours had invaded my life. I felt like I could hear them talking about my injury. It was as if they had heard and seen what had happened to me. I felt like I was being watched and that they had some type of signal that was allowing them to invade my home.

The neighbours across the stream had a karaoke system and I could hear them singing and criticising me in their songs. I also heard the neighbours behind my house arguing. It sounded like there was domestic violence occurring.

Hearing all these voices was both disturbing and frightening. Why could I hear them and how could they hear me? I told my housemate about this but he didn't understand as only I could hear these voices.

I felt like I was being watched every second of the day and being criticised for what I wore, what I ate and everything I did. I could not escape from it. From the minute I woke in the morning, they would start with me. The worst was going for a shower so I started to bath rather than to shower and put a small-lit candle in the corner of the bathroom hoping they could not see me anymore. When I was in my lounge or dining room, I would put all the lights off and use a single candle in the hope that they could not see me, but the badgering and comments continued. I decided to close all the air vents with paper, thinking that they had perhaps installed cameras in the air vents. I was totally paranoid.

I started talking back to them. It was annoying and consuming me. I can just imagine, if someone had seen me talking to myself like this, they would have thought I had gone completely mad, but it felt so real. Everything I did, I automatically gave explanations for what I was doing in the hope that these 'people' would leave me alone. I now realise that my mind had been taken over by demonic forces.

Things continued to get worse.

One evening, whilst lying on the couch, I felt something different, as if I was being played with sexually. It seemed like they were using some sort of machine (a laser or type of ultrasound machine) pinpointing my private part.

I didn't know what to do or who to speak to. I thought no-one would believe me. I put metal dishes or anything made from steel in front of my stomach to see whether this would maybe stop but it didn't work. I constantly felt that they could see everything that I could see and I felt it was impossible to hide details away from them.

I was also tormented by these 'creatures' who were trying to scare me. They were in demon form. They could enter through the air vents or windows if left slightly open. I felt like they wanted to kill me.

These 'creatures/demons' would come into my room, stand right in front of my face, checking to see whether I was breathing or not. I would lie in my bed trying not to breathe or show any signs of life.

This would carry on every evening and sometimes all night. I couldn't get proper rest and I lost so much weight from all the stress.

One morning, I was made to feel and believe that I was having a heart attack. I believed that a doctor was on his way but, after what felt like hours had passed, I realised no-one was coming. It felt like this was D-Day. Everything became dead quiet – no wind, no sound of birds, nothing – complete silence.

Something told me that they were on their way to come and crucify me and that everything was already set up at the back of the house for this event.

I went outside to check and there it was – a pile of planks stacked, some pieces having nails in them.

Fortunately, my housemate arrived back and I told him I had to get away from the house. I was in a complete state of panic and fear, realising I was in trouble. I made a call to my mother asking her for our church minister's telephone number. I called him and I explained what was happening to me. He was unable to see me as he was going on leave but said he would contact his son, Marius, to help me.

I received a call from Marius and he then invited me

to meet with Mary-Ann, Clint and himself. I met with them and explained all the events. Clint and Mary-Ann immediately understood what was happening and suggested I come back the next evening as they needed to contact a friend, René, who was experienced in deliverance ministry, to pray with me. The following night we met again. René joined us at their house. They all listened to me and then prayed for me. Soon after this meeting, I also received a call from our new church minister, Annetjie, as she had heard that I needed help.

She said I had to meet her at the church, which I did, and I told her what was happening to me. Annetjie managed to book us into a B&B across town and gave me the address. Whilst driving there, I tried to keep my eyes half-closed as I drove, hoping 'they' wouldn't see where I was driving to. I arrived at the B&B. Annetjie had to go out as she had another appointment to attend to. After about 10 minutes, I heard a loud noise and a terrible aggressive voice right outside our door. I just held the Bible, started praying and froze whilst sitting on the bed.

When Annetjie returned, we decided to read the Bible. We both opened our Bibles at exactly the same place, Psalm 91, our protection Psalm, and it was confirmation that God was watching out for me.

The next day, Clint and Mary-Ann came to see us and we all prayed together. From here, I was later admitted to hospital because there were no openings at Oatlands. A few days later, Mary-Ann messaged me, saying there was an opening for me at Oatlands and they were coming to fetch me.

I thank the Lord for sending Mary-Ann and Clint to help me. They ensured I was admitted to Oatlands. They drove me there where I stayed for 17 days.

I did not really understand what the whole purpose of my being at Oatlands was at the time, but today I am thankful I was there. These demons followed me there but they had to finally flee as I started filling myself up with the Word of God – reading my Bible, calling on Jesus to help me and I was being covered in prayer. I joined a Bible Study group at Oatlands. Mary-Ann and Clint kept me in their prayers the entire time and they both kept in contact with me.

Mary-Ann, Clint, Warren and Marius went to the house where I live. They anointed and prayed over the house.

By the time I was released from Oatlands, I could not hear these 'people'. When I arrived back at my home, I still felt a bit shaken, but everything seemed normal again. My peace was being restored and I was getting back to my old self.

If it were not for these very special people who all helped me through this, I don't know what would have happened to me.

All I can say is that God is great and uses people like Mary-Ann, Clint and Annetjie, like angels, to help people like me who experienced a full-blown demonic attack on my life and they understood spiritual warfare.

I recommitted my life to Jesus and repented of all my sins. I was set free from the demonic oppression

I had allowed to enter my life. Praise the Lord! He would never let one of His sheep, who believes in Him, disappear.

by Hannelie Koning

The Lord sends us on assignments and puts people in our paths for us to guide and lead in His ways. We are vessels at His disposal and we all need to be obedient to His calling and to be bold and courageous when He calls us to action. I have on many occasions told people about not getting involved in crystal healing and asking for protection from dead ancestors. The Lord has sent people to our home and into our lives who wear bracelets and strings around their wrists, allowing the enemy access into their lives, without them even realising and knowing this. We have been privileged to have witnessed transformations as God's Hand was actively working in their lives. We pray the Lord will continue to send people into our lives whom He wants us to guide or assist. Wherever He leads we will follow and we will continue to see His hand in things all around us.

I am constantly in awe at how He has brought people into our lives, where we are led to give counsel and offer guidance to, one such example would be that, due to Covid, we have had to order a lot of items online. We had a gentleman from Takealot deliver one day. My eyes were drawn to his bracelet and I asked him what it was. He said, "Crystals, healing crystals". I immediately began to give him a brief rundown of Katherine's and our testimony and he left without saying too much. A few days later, he arrived back at our home with another delivery and the first thing I observed was that the bracelet was missing. He asked if I had noticed something. I replied that it was the first thing I had noticed. After he had left our home on the day I had spoken to him, he said he had been convicted and had got rid of it. He told me he was starting to read his Bible. A few days later, Clint met him and was led to pray with him in the driveway.

On another occasion, we were going to visit a colleague of Clint's in Richards Bay. On our way there, he called to say he wasn't feeling well. As we were nearly there, we decided to continue with the trip. That night, we stopped at a restaurant for dinner. The owner told us how accident-prone she was and how she had broken nearly every bone in her body. Just a few weeks prior, she had broken her nose for the second time and these events had been happening to her for years.

Whilst we were talking to her, another gentleman at the counter recognised her and said the last time he had seen her, she had been working for Game Stores. She had been on crutches with a broken leg. She couldn't believe that the gentleman had even recognised her because that had been years ago. This opened a conversation where Clint asked her about the necklace she was wearing. He told her to take off the crystal healing necklace as it had attachments to the demonic world. We don't always realise what we invite into our lives when endorsing such items. She immediately removed her necklace and told us her mom was a Bible-bashing Christian. She had grown up in a Christian home with a Christian upbringing but said she was no longer very involved in all that. We laughed and said we were not Bible bashers, nor religious, but we sure do love Jesus.

This was no coincidence that the gentleman was there at that exact moment when we were about to leave, that he had recognised her after so many years and he was also professing his love for Jesus. I think her Bible-bashing mom had been praying fervently for her daughter to turn back to Jesus and the Lord was sending people into her life to water the seeds that had been planted.

I think of Clint and how he used to be when he hated his drive to Durban. He has been travelling from Pietermaritzburg to Durban, approximately a 50-minute drive, for over 20 years. Now he doesn't have enough hours on the road to listen to his audio Bible and enjoying praise and worship music whilst on route to his office.

I laugh because, a few years earlier, he would swear under his breath at one of the managers who would pick him up on occasions while she blasted her Christian music which drove him absolutely mad. Yet now he is the one blasting the Christian music. Again, God's sense of humour never ceases to amaze us. Clint is on fire for Jesus and I don't think much time goes by during the day that he doesn't talk about our King. I love him so much and thank God that he chose Clint for me. He has truly made us one.

Mark 10:8
and the two shall become one flesh; so then they are no longer two, but one flesh.

Genesis 2:24
Therefore a man shall leave his father and mother and be joined to his wife, and they shall become one flesh.

We often discuss and agree how God has united us and truly has made us one. In the big things and the little things, He is constantly revealing Himself to us. One of the first examples of this was not long after we had been saved. Clint went for a swim in our pool after taking the dogs for a run and he said that, as he stood in the pool, he scooped up a bee in his hands. He looked at the dead bee and thought that God could bring this bee to life. After pondering on this, he threw the bee over the wall.

Later that morning, I was suntanning with Kelsey and, when I stepped into the pool, I saw a dead bee. I picked it up and thought, 'God, You can bring this bee back to life' but then I felt guilty and thought I should not test God like that and threw the bee on the grass. Later that afternoon, Clint relayed his bee story to me and I told him I had done the exact same thing. We both laughed. The next morning, when Clint came back from his run and was filling up the dogs' water bowls, he stood up. I was in the kitchen and we both locked eyes. As we looked at each other, a bee was flying between us – we knew God was talking to us and that He had made the two one.

After visiting a friend for a cup of coffee, it was laid on my heart to pray for one of the couples with whom we had been on holiday in Israel. This doesn't normally happen to me but I was obedient and prayed over the couple, specifically for the husband, my entire car ride home. Later that evening, I told Clint I had prayed for this couple and he said he had sent the same chap a message of encouragement that day. He showed me his phone and it was at the exact same time I was praying. Clint never sends him messages, so we were both blown away by this – confirmation of how God has made us one. It breaks my heart to say this, but that same gentleman went for a cycle one evening during lockdown and never returned home. We continue to pray and trust in the Lord.

The Lord speaks to us through His Word. Clint, on one of his early morning runs, was thinking about a scripture which came into his mind – Jeremiah 17:7. He wanted to look it up in his Bible when he came home but it was in his car so he left it. Later, he looked at my WhatsApp status and guess what it was.

Jeremiah 17:7
Blessed is the man who trusts in the Lord, and whose hope is the Lord.

I had sat for quite a while that morning asking God about scripture verses. I then saw someone had sent me that scripture the previous night and I thought that was the perfect update. When Clint saw the verse, he smiled and said the two are one. We were collecting Clint's new car that morning in Durban and the way it all worked out, we just knew that God's Hand was in it. We are truly blessed because we truly do trust in the Lord.

John 1:16
And of His fullness we have all received, and grace for grace.

One Sunday morning, we were asked to assist Clint's Bible Study host by collecting his vehicle from Justin, his employee. He had asked Clint to please also pray with Justin as he was struggling with alcoholism and drugs. Clint asked if I would go with him after he returned from his morning jog. Whilst Clint was jogging, Warren arrived at our home and said he would go with Clint. We all prayed together for the Lord to go before them and for their safety and peace as the owner of the house had several Boerboels. As they drove off, I immediately went into my prayer closet and put on praise and worship music. I looked down on my phone and the words from Isaiah 55 came up. I immediately picked up my Bible and began to pray Isaiah 55 over Clint and Warren.

Clint arrived home with no vehicle and he immediately began to relay the story of what had transpired and how amazing God was for putting people in the path of those who could relate to one another's stories. Clint had said things had not gone according to plan and that Justin whom they were meant to get the car from wasn't home. They landed up talking to and praying with Justin's dad. Clint said he did not say anything and just listened. He smiled to himself thinking that the Lord's ways are not our ways and that His thoughts are not our thoughts. We were sitting at the dining room table and he opened his WhatsApp. He looked at a friend's WhatsApp status and said "Oh my goodness". This is exactly what I was thinking earlier. He showed me the status. It was Isaiah 55:8 *"For My thoughts are not your thoughts, nor are your ways My ways', says the Lord"*. He was shocked as that was exactly what he had just been thinking earlier. I, of course, immediately jumped up and grabbed my Bible, saying that was the scripture that the Holy Spirit lead me to pray over them when they had left to collect the car. We both smiled at each other and thanked the Lord for His confirmation.

Later that morning Clint and I went back to fetch the vehicle from Justin. We stood in the driveway listening to Justin's mom relaying what had transpired the previous night. Justin had taken his girlfriend and his son out for dinner, it had been his son's birthday. Justin had been using cocaine most of that day and he had far too many drinks at dinner, so he was not able to recall how he had arrived home. After listening to Justin and his mom, I noticed that Justin was shaking like a leaf, suffering from withdrawals, so I prayed for him right there.

A few months later Justin told us that he had contemplated committing suicide that very day we came to see him. He said after we left he was tired and angry and he cried out to the Lord for help, he stated he was done and that he gave it all to the Lord. He said that peace and a warm feeling came over him, something he had never experienced before, and from that day onwards his life changed. The many years of alcohol and drug abuse was finally over, strongholds had been broken. Since then he married his girlfriend, who also committed her life to Jesus on their wedding day and shortly thereafter they were both baptized in our swimming pool. Watching this couple grow in the Lord has been a true blessing to us and Justin is now on fire for Jesus.

There have been endless examples of sending messages at the same time or reminding each other of things simultaneously. We are in awe of our King and what He has done in our lives.

God reminds us in all kinds of situations how He hears our cries and prayers. We had prayed and fasted for Kelsey's return from the UK during covid. My sister in Christ, Bridget, had sent me a message that God had told her that we would see Kelsey in October. To be truly honest, we thought she had got it wrong because we had planned for November as the borders were still closed and there was no sign of the borders opening for international travel. But God is faithful to His promises and she returned on 9th October 2020. That is not to say that the enemy didn't come to rattle us. Kelsey was extremely sick a few days prior to her flight home and she had to pray hard that she would not even cough when she went for her covid test which, thank the Lord, was negative. We knew it would be.

A few days before her flight home, Emirates Airline announced that, due to new rules and regulations, they were unable to fly into Durban or South Africa. We had to really put our faith in the Lord that the mess would be sorted out, and sorted out quickly, which He did. At Heathrow Airport, they did not want to accept Kelsey's covid test as they said it had expired. However, after she explained nicely to the assistant how the hours worked, she was able to proceed and board the plane home. There was a song that was laid on my heart for Kelsey called *You're still God* by Philippa Hanna. I cried when I listened to it and I sent it to her in August 2020. I knew it was a song for her. On the morning we went to collect her from the airport, the lady I mentioned earlier, who played her Christian music when she used to fetch Clint, sent this exact song to Clint as we drove out of our driveway and she actually never sends him songs. It was confirmation that God was in control and I had tears in my eyes.

We took Kelsey to Shalom Ministries on 18th October 2020 and Pastor Kevin's sermon was brilliant. It was about how he had a stone in his shoe that morning. A small tiny stone can make your journey so uncomfortable and he reminded us of how the enemy is bent on making your journey difficult and that we all have struggles. He spoke about some of the great men and women in the Bible who had their fair share of trials, tribulations and struggles and I truly felt the message spoke to Kelsey. Our poor child has had her fair share of health issues over the past years but we are trusting God for her complete healing and restoration. We will continue to pray and fast for her breakthrough and we will continue to stand on the scripture God gave me – Luke 8:50. As I sit here typing this story, He has given me another scripture as confirmation.

Psalm 107:20-22
[20] He sent His word and healed them, and delivered them from their destructions. [21] Oh, that men would

give thanks to the LORD for His goodness, and for His wonderful works to the children of men! ²²Let them sacrifice the sacrifices of thanksgiving, and declare His works with rejoicing.

When Pastor Kevin completed his sermon, he said he would like to play us something on the big screen. The song You're still God started playing. Clint and I glanced at each other with tears streaming down our faces. Lord, You are amazing! We love You and worship only You.

Prayer and fasting are an act of obedience and Christians should take time to do this. Our daily walk should be filled with His Word, praise and worship and be in prayer and, if called to fast, we should be obedient to the calling. Fasting is a powerful practice which helps us draw closer to God and helps us remember that we can rely on Him. The Bible is full of examples of men and women who fasted. Jesus makes a lot of powerful promises in His Word. He promises that we can ask for anything in His Name and He will do it.

John 14:13-14
¹³And whatever you ask in My name, that I will do, that the Father may be glorified in the Son. ¹⁴If you ask anything in My name, I will do it.

He promises to never turn away anyone who turns to Him.

John 6:37
All that the Father gives Me will come to Me, and the one who comes to Me I will by no means cast out.

He promises to have compassion for us, no matter what our shortcomings are.

Mark 2:17
When Jesus heard it, He said to them, "Those who are well have no need of a physician, but those who are sick. I did not come to call the righteous, but sinners, to repentance."

These promises require one to exercise their faith. True faith will demonstrate itself through actions and the above practices will build our faith, ensuring that we are aligning ourselves to Jesus so we can experience His fullness, His protection, His provision and His power in our lives.

Let us first repent of anything in our lives which is not pleasing to God – things that do not honour Him. The Lord is gracious to forgive us and welcomes us back home with open arms. Let us turn from our wicked ways and He is faithful and just in pushing back evil in our lives. He will help us overcome any obstacles in our way. Let us fight the good fight with prayer, worship and being in His Word constantly. I find it quite disappointing how many Christians do not truly know the Word of God and seldom read their Bibles. It sits on a shelf or in a drawer collecting dust and the devil smiles as he knows how powerful the Word is. That's why it's called our sword.

The devil keeps us so busy that we find it difficult to make time for God and His Word. His Word is very clear though in Matthew 6:33: *"But seek first the kingdom of God and His righteousness, and all these things shall be added to you."*

As Christians, we need to activate the spiritual weapons of prayer and intercession and use the power of the Scriptures – our sword to decree the works of satan powerless in our lives. God wants us to experience His power and His love, to talk to Him and cry out to Him and

I promise you He will show up for you as He did for us. There is no other name that has power to save but the Name of Jesus.

The enemy wants you to depend on yourself or on others. He does not want you or me to have an intimate relationship with Jesus. He does not want us to inherit the Kingdom of God because he has tasted and seen this kingdom and by no means wants us to get there. However, we have powerful weapons at our disposal and, when we focus on God and praise Him, the enemy runs for the hills.

We are often asked how these demons left us and I can honestly say that, the more we filled ourselves up with God's Word, the Holy Bible, and the more we spoke to God, they had no option but to flee. The enemies' lies were shattered and broken into pieces. We were set free and were no longer slaves to sin – born-again children of God!

God also protects us and will not allow us to be tempted beyond what we can handle.

> **1 Corinthians 10:13**
> *No temptation has overtaken you except such as is common to man; but God is faithful, who will not allow you to be tempted beyond what you are able, but with the temptation will also make the way of escape, that you may be able to bear it.*

I won a trip to Amsterdam in August 2019, a competition which Sharné and I had entered, so we were both super-excited and ecstatic about the win. The entire trip was just a couple of days and the itinerary even made Clint think he would need to cover us in prayer. We would be on yachts with people from all over the world who had also won and the party would not end as late-night clubbing was the order of the day.

Clint anointed us with oil and prayed protection over us on the afternoon we left from the Pietermaritzburg airport. Things didn't go as per our plans. As we reached the international travel counter in Johannesburg, we were asked for our passports. We handed them our South African ones with the document which had been emailed to us about visas from the company. It's so crazy because I have travelled so much in the past and normally would take both my passports but not this time. This time, I took out our other passports and said we wouldn't need them. The document we thought was a travel visa we received from the company was in fact insufficient and they would not let us board the plane. Sharné was mortified and devastated as she could not believe it. I, on the other hand, was calm and said, "God doesn't want us on this trip, Sharné". I knew in my heart that He had said it would be too soon to put me in a situation where I would be surrounded by drinking and partygoers – something I was all too familiar with. I have not been drunk since the day I gave my life to the Lord. It's an absolute miracle that He took the desire to drink away from me in a flash but the devil comes to tempt. He comes to rob, steal and destroy.

I remember clearly the organiser of the trip telling me he couldn't believe how calm I was about the situation. He still joked and said he had seen that movie where the plane goes down. I knew it wasn't that. I knew the real reason why we were not going on that trip. My niece was kind enough to fetch us from the airport and we flew home the following day. After many tears were shed, Sharné finally agreed that maybe it was for the best that we were not on the trip. Sitting in Church that Sunday, my phone started going crazy with pictures of all the people on the trip as they had formed a WhatsApp group. I showed Clint all the pics on the group. They were sitting having drinks in the red-light district in Amsterdam and I said, "Now where do you think God wanted me?" We both smiled at each other. Not long after that, Sharné and I were blessed with a trip to Cape Town to a non-alcoholic festival. How great is our God!

Over the past few days, I have been praying for God to reveal to me anything in me that is unpleasing to Him. I woke up the one morning feeling sick and queasy. It felt like I had food poisoning. I had sent a message on my work group that I would be in late as I wasn't feeling great. The Holy Spirit led me to have communion early that morning and the scripture came to me about abiding in Him and His words abiding in me.

> **John 15:4-6**
> ^{4}*Abide in Me, and I in you. As the branch cannot bear fruit of itself, unless it abides in the vine, neither can you, unless you abide in Me.*^{5}*"I am the vine, you are the branches. He who abides in Me, and I in him, bears much fruit; for without Me you can do nothing.* ^{6}*If anyone does not abide in Me, he is cast out as a branch and is withered; and they gather them and throw them into the fire, and they are burned.*

I had communion and prayed for God's healing Hands. I was at work by 7 am, feeling much better. We had our usual daily prayer meeting and my work colleague, Sibongile, read the scripture about not coveting your neighbour's things. It's the 10th commandment and I didn't think too much of it because I'm not in want of my neighbour's things. I usually feel really happy for people who are doing well but, as we started praying, it was as if God was chastising me. He challenged me to look at myself. I was coveting my neighbour's things. I was slowly becoming very angry and indeed jealous of my boss and two of my staff members who were working from home because of Covid, yet receiving full pay because of their comorbidity issues. It was starting to drive me nuts. These staff members each had their own offices and yet still stayed away. God showed me that morning that was not of Him and I needed to repent of that. I knew right there and then I was in the exact place where He wanted me, on my knees, praying fervently with Sibongile. We stood up and praised the Lord, thanking Him for our health and the blessing of being able to come to work, to be able to gather as sisters in Christ, truly grateful for all the blessings He has poured into our lives.

I made a booking for Clint, Sharné and myself to go to the Happy Wanderers Resort for the weekend of 12th March 2021 to celebrate Clint's 48th birthday at the beach. Sharné had asked Clint if the resort had Wi-Fi. He said there was, not even giving it a second thought because, really, we are living in the 21st Century. Surely there is Wi-Fi or 3G everywhere – well, so he thought. She needed to work and had an assignment to complete. Unfortunately, when we arrived, Clint was shocked that there was no Wi-Fi and the 3G only worked in the pub. He was practically in denial and said there at least had to be 3G working in our room. Sadly, there wasn't and we headed back home as we couldn't expect Sharné to be in the pub the entire weekend. The receptionist at the resort was kind enough to slot us into another weekend (16th April 2021). She booked us into a smaller room as Sharné said that she wouldn't be joining us. At that stage, it was the first available weekend and we didn't even realise that that date would be our wedding anniversary weekend, but God did.

When we arrived home and I started unpacking all the

goodies back into the fridge, I thought about the number plate I had seen on Thursday morning and again on Friday morning – Psalm 91 – and I instantly thought about the powerful testimony we had recently watched on YouTube. It was the testimony of the father of one of Kelsey's friends on how God had moved in his life and how a shark had bitten right though his paddle ski. I thought about what I had first read on the pamphlet when we arrived at Happy Wanderers Resort – 'no swimming in the sea', and that had upset me terribly. One of the staff had said it would be fine to swim as we had taken our three boogie boards with us. The area is renowned for its sharks and the evidence was in all the photos of sharks that had been caught in the area. These pictures hung on all the pub walls.

A friend from work, Diana, had also called me that Friday morning. I hadn't heard from her in months and she wanted to ask me if I believed that God speaks to people though dreams. I told her I believe He definitely does. He spoke to many people in the Bible through dreams and visions. She proceeded to tell me her dream – she was at a cottage on the beach. I still thought about the cottage we were going into which was right on the beach. She said there was a ship in the distance that was sinking and there was black, thick stuff like oil running from the ship. She could see it running through the sea, then onto the sand and finally into the cottage. Then she woke up. Thinking back to her phone call while I was still unpacking all our luggage, I now truly believed that God didn't want us there on that weekend. I was happy and content knowing that God was in control.

We finally went for our beach weekend on 16th April and had planned to set a lot of time aside to start going through the book I was writing – this book you are now reading. However, to be honest, we didn't get much done as we spent a lot of time sharing our testimony with others there. It was an amazing weekend and one we will never forget. As we sat on our little verandah right on the beach on the Friday evening, enjoying the sunset and braaiing, I noticed a man in a wheelchair go past our unit and, in my mind, I immediately thought about God's healing power. Later that evening, I discussed with Clint how I was feeling and he said he also thought the same thing. I'm sure it is something that, at one stage or another, goes through every believer's mind – God's healing power.

Upon waking on the Saturday morning, I had a nagging in my spirit about the man in the wheelchair and asked Clint if we could pray about it. We sat on the bed and I prayed that, if it was God's will for us to pray for the man in the wheelchair, He would bring him right to our doorstep. We had breakfast and then proceeded to go for a long walk on the beach. To my surprise, there was another man in a buggy wheelchair on the beach, fishing. Again, I thought about God's healing power and, all of a sudden, I heard a loud voice shouting "Thomas". Some guy on the beach was throwing a rugby ball and I immediately turned to Clint, saying, "Clint, I am not a 'doubting Thomas'". Clint asked if I was thinking about the man in the wheelchair and I said I was.

After about an hour's walk, we headed back to our room. We couldn't have been there for more than a few minutes. Clint was in the bathroom when I looked out and, right there in front of our door, were both the men in wheelchairs. I could barely speak and tried to call Clint. His eyes were as big as saucers. I quickly moved outside in total shock and disbelief. I mean, what were the chances that both these men would now meet each other for the first time right at our front door. There were 25 ground floor flats and we were in number 6. I was staring at these poor men so intently, not quite knowing what to do. I was unaware that Clint was hiding behind the curtains, sweating bullets and thinking to himself, "Lord, am I going to have to say to them, 'get up and walk in the Name of Jesus?'"

It's one thing to say you will pray for something but a whole different thing following through with it. He said he looked down onto the small table to his right and his eyes caught the word *'faith'* on the *Faith like Potatoes* book he had brought down to the beach with us. He said he didn't even know why he had brought it with him because he had read the book, but now, he was staring at the word *'faith'*. He picked up the book and just opened it. The words 'Why not do it now?' jumped out at him from the page. In total shock, he came to sit outside with me. He looked pale and, quite frankly, like a stunned lizard. I told him in a joking manner that this was when women must be silent as mentioned in the Bible. In a small voice he said, "Excuse me, guys" and, just like that, they both went their separate ways and disappeared. Trying to fully understand what had just happened and both of us in shock, we decided we had to be obedient to the Holy Spirit. We had heard the one man's name was Shaun and that he was staying in unit 25, so we decided we would go and ask if we could pray for him. We took a slow walk down to unit 25. It was the last unit and, as we approached, we could see Shaun in his wheelchair. My eyes caught sight of other people sitting on the verandah and I felt a little bit of stress creep in – I cannot lie. Then Clint said to me, "Mary-Ann, isn't that our godchild, Amy, and isn't that our friend, Dee?" To my absolute shock, it was. We hadn't seen them in 20 years. I gave Dee a hug and became very emotional seeing them.

We explained how we had prayed that morning and that is how we were led to come and pray for Shaun. God had a plan all along. Dee said she had told Shaun a few days prior that she was wondering what had happened to her friends, Clint and Mary-Ann, and there we were in front of her. Shaun said that, the way I had been staring at him earlier, he thought I may have recognised him or that I knew him. He told us that, over the years, many Christians had offered to pray for him and he had always accepted, as one never knows when God will move.

What an amazing couple. Shaun was Dee's first love. We shared our testimonies with one another and Clint and I prayed for Dee for her multiple sclerosis. She is also in a wheelchair. We also prayed for Shaun. We know that God is the Healer and the great Physician in whom we trust. Dee told me she had brought a book to the beach, having no idea why, because she had already read it, but now she knew why. It was for me. Isn't our God so amazing that He orchestrated a meeting with our godchild and put us back in her life after 20 years. We can only now be the godparents she deserves and we ask the Lord to lead us in all His ways.

Here is her testimony in her own words:

My journey with God has been quite a roller coaster. I grew up in what I knew was a 'Christian' home. My grandparents on both sides considered themselves Christians and I would often go to Sunday school with my dad's parents. However, I only realised, when I was about 13 years old, what it really meant to be Christian and to have a relationship with God and Jesus.

When I was 12-years-old, in my last year of primary school, my mother's partner at the time started sexually abusing me. He had groomed me right from the day we moved in with him at 6 years of age. While it was happening, I didn't feel great about it but I also knew I loved him and thought he loved me. He would threaten me that, if I spoke about it, he would kick my mom, brother and me out of his house and we would have no place to go. Being young, I believed him and I was scared of him, not questioning if what he said would really happen, so I allowed it to carry on.

When I was 13, I attended Grace College. This was where my journey with God began.

I cannot thank Him enough for opening paths up for me to attend this school as it was my foundation to my relationship with God.

I gave my life to the Lord at a school camp when I was 13-years-old.

At Grace College we would have a compulsory subject about biblical studies which introduced me to the Bible and Jesus. I loved this subject and looked forward to it each week and soon started studying and reading the Bible at home too. I began praying to God every night and sometimes found myself talking to Him during the day.

One day, when I was about 14 years-old in Grade 9, I was sitting on a bench after school waiting for my mom's partner to fetch me. There was a voice in my head that addressed me and said I could no longer be treated the way I was being treated. I had felt uncomfortable about the sexual abuse for a long time but didn't know how to go about addressing it.

I remember the voice telling me that I needed to talk directly to my mom's partner to put a stop to the abuse, telling him I was not comfortable and didn't want it. At that time, I thought I was crazy; maybe just 'talking to myself' or 'hearing what I wanted to hear', but I did it anyway.

My mom's partner was a bit late that day and, when he arrived, I climbed onto the front passenger seat, as usual, but kept to myself. Immediately, he started with his charming ways – asking me if I wanted to go get a milkshake or a coffee on our way home, while placing his hand on my leg closest to him. I thanked him and told him I needed to get home to do my homework. He took me to the shops anyway. When we arrived, I told him I would stay in the car while he went in. When he got back, I told him we needed to talk. I told him I no longer wanted him to continue with the abuse and that I had found God who had shown me how wrong it was. He laughed at me and drove us home.

About two weeks later, he and my mom had a fallout and we moved to my grandparents' house.

I continued my education at Grace College until June, when my mom got engaged and later married one of her high school sweethearts with whom she had always stayed in contact with. We moved to Richards Bay where I attended Richards Bay Christian School but, unfortunately, with the move and all that had happened, I lost contact with God. I had stopped praying and reading the Bible and focused more on trying to fit in and make friends.

When we moved into the house in Richards Bay with

my new new stepdad and his son who was 19-years-old at the time, there were things I just couldn't make sense of.

My stepbrother was having a gap year and belonged to the church band. I remember no-one was really allowed in his room, including my mom or our nanny, and, when we were allowed in his room, all I wanted was to get out. I used to feel so freaked out and uncomfortable in there but couldn't understand why or what gave me the feeling.

His room was always dark – he never opened his black curtains, he had weird posters all over his black walls that had pictures of the ram's head, stars and upside-down crosses.

A few months after we moved in, my stepbrother joined a 'new-age' band and they made a music video which he was very proud of and showed it to us. It was heavy metal, very dark and full of smoke. I couldn't understand what they were 'singing' (screaming!) and the other guys in the band all had their shirts off, showing their tattoos of the ram and upside-down crosses. One day whilst my mom was in his room cleaning the linen she saw an Ouija board as well as red and black candles under his bed.

A few months later, my stepbrother moved out and, after a good clean of his room, I decided to move in. This was when the battle began...

Every time my stepbrother visited our house, pictures of him would fall off our walls after he left. Bad things started happening at home and I was too scared to talk out about it because I felt embarrassed and scared no-one would believe me.

The week after my stepbrother moved out, I had settled in nicely and put my posters up on the wall. I remember the words on them being 'Peace', 'Love', 'Joy', etc. I painted my walls a deep lilac to brighten the room a bit compared to the black walls.

It was after the paint had dried that we noticed a smell. It is so difficult to explain what it smelt like – all I can liken it to is death or sulphur. We cleaned the room again, top to bottom, inside all the cupboards and everywhere you can think of. Eventually the smell faded away.

Every night I was woken up by the feeling of something pushing down on my chest and I felt like I couldn't breathe. I couldn't move my body at all and couldn't shout for help. I remember shivering and shaking because I was so scared. I eventually was able to move my head slightly for me to see what time it was on my alarm clock next to my bed and it was 1.55 am – every single night.

Then, one night, I saw this figure standing at the foot of my bed. I started crying. I couldn't make out what it was or who it was or even if it had a face, but it was dressed in a black robe with a hood hanging over its head and all I could see was its eyes staring at me. When I was able to move again, I ran to my mom's room and told her everything. I felt so stupid and like such a baby but something was not right.

I then started feeling too scared to walk passed the room. If I had to get anything from the other side of the house, I would run passed the room because I felt this cold presence and it freaked me out.

After weeks of sleeping on a mattress in my mom's room, my mom spoke to my stepdad's mother who is a Christian who has been studying the Bible for decades. She also did a lot of research about spiritual warfare. She advised my mom that we should pray over our house and go around to each room, pray over it and anoint the door with oil in the pattern of a cross.

I remember these 24 hours like it was yesterday.

It was the first time I picked up the Bible since leaving Grace College. My mom and I walked around the house and anointed each room after praying Psalm 91.

That afternoon, my mom and I were chatting on her bed. We had all three dogs with us. My brother was in his bedroom and my stepdad in the garage. Suddenly, there was a huge shattering noise that came from the kitchen. It sounded like an explosion of shattered glass. I ran down the passage, shouting at my brother and asking him what he had broken, only to find he was in his room. I walked slowly into the kitchen where a crystal ashtray had shattered. But it was near impossible as there was no-one else in the house and the ashtray was in the middle of a corner shelf, not near an edge to fall. I began cleaning up the mess when I realised the pieces of broken crystal were in perfect little squares. Each and every one of them. I ran to my mom and told her what happened – we were absolutely petrified!

That night, after eventually falling asleep in my own

room (my stepbrother's old room), I was woken up by ALL my posters falling down. I immediately opened my Bible to Psalm 23 and prayed the prayer out loud about ten times when my Bible was shut closed supernaturally. I was so scared, I ran to my mom's room and slept there for the rest of the night.

In the morning, it was like nothing had happened except when we went into the lounge where my mom had a photo-collaged wall and every single photo of my stepbrother had fallen down.

Since that day, we have not experienced anything like this. I am just so grateful that God was by my side every step of the way to guide me and protect me. I would never have been able to get through either one of my negative experiences without His help and His Word.

After doing research and chatting to spiritual leaders and members of the church, we now know that the shattering of the crystal ashtray, the posters in my room and the photos of my stepbrother falling down and my Bible being shut closed was the work of an evil spirit who had been upset with us for getting God involved. It was the spirit's way of telling us it was leaving.

Although these were both very traumatic experiences, I wouldn't change it for the world, as they have led me closer to God and strengthened my relationship with Jesus.

Whenever I feel weary or unsafe, I pray Psalm 23:

1. The Lord is my Shepherd, I lack nothing.
2. He makes me lie down in green pastures, He

leads me beside quiet waters.
3. He refreshes my soul. He guides me along the right paths for His name's sake.
4. Even though I walk through the valley of the shadow of death, I will fear no evil, for You are with me; Your rod and Your staff, they comfort me.
5. You prepare a table before me in the presence of my enemies. You anoint my head with oil; my cup overflows.
6. Surely Your goodness and love will follow me all the days of my life, and I will dwell in the house of the Lord forever.

by Amy Hempel

Later that day, we spoke to the other gentleman in the wheelchair and his lovely wife. He had been an upcoming rugby star, but a car accident, while in his 20s, left him paralysed and cut short his career. I was humbled at how content he was, surrounded by his beautiful family. We shared stories and he told us about a new venture he wanted to go into, selling eggs with his dad. We told them we would pray for them and for their business, which we did, and I trust the Lord will bless them.

This was such an amazing weekend, we also had the opportunity to meet a couple who was staying in the unit right next to us, after initial introductions it wasn't long before we started to share our testimonies. Karen opened up to us about how she had got involved in the Native American Religion and Spirituality and how this then wreaked havoc in her life.

Here is her testimony in her own words:
A FREE SPIRIT

After sixteen years of marriage to an atheist and a compulsive liar, I finally got the courage to leave. I wanted to be a free spirit. My understanding of a free spirit at that time was to do what I wanted, have no limits nor boundaries, and do what made me happy. Looking back, I realized I was in bondage, and the more I wanted to be free the more bound I became.

I remarried, and my husband and I loved nature. We became interested in the ways of the Native American Indians (being more interested in the creation rather than the Creator). We blessed one another with rituals and forefather blessings. (This was an open door to the occult, but we did not realize it at the time.) Our farm house soon became decorated with posters and memorabilia imported from North America. We were Idolizing the Native American Indian Warriors for their courage and love for nature. Needless to say, the first three years of our marriage was a disaster as we fought endlessly and my husband drank heavily. We even got trapped in pornography. The devil was having a field day trying to destroy us and killing everything we had. (John 10:10)

Our lives changed drastically when the director, Regardt van den Bergh, came to Greytown to shoot the movie 'Faith like Potatoes." For the first time ever, we experienced the love of Jesus by watching the crew and actors. We witnessed the fruit of the Holy Spirit amongst the crew, and we desperately wanted to be part of that. Our repentance and revival started once we denounced all we believed in and we burnt all the tribal memorabilia. We were at last set free. A FREE SPIRIT.

We accepted Jesus into our lives, and were baptized at Shalom Church in the middle of winter in a reservoir. By being baptized, we made a public announcement that we had received Jesus as our Saviour, but we were not filled by the Holy Spirit. We started studying every book on witchcraft and how the enemy works as we wanted to make sure never to be trapped in the enemy's snare again (Hosea 4v1). Yes, he tried many times to set a trap to ensnare us, but because of our knowledge, we were saved. The Lord had much molding to do, and He started peeling us like an onion – layer by layer. Our tribulations taught us how to draw closer to Him. The more we drew closer to Him, the more we got to understand His love for us. This process took years. God placed ordinary people in our lives to help us grow through seasons. Uncle Angus was one of them.

After 17 years of marriage, my husband was diagnosed with cancer. He refused treatment and passed away 2 years later. He lived his life loving and serving the Lord to the end. He was free from bondages, free from alcohol and smoking abuse. He died a FREE SPIRIT in Christ Jesus alone.

by Karen Meyer

Chapter 11

Touching Lives

My daughter, Kelsey, and I had the privilege of going on a mission trip with One Life Church to Ingwavuma on the KZN North Coast – a seven-hour journey from Pietermaritzburg. It was our first mission trip and the feeling of going out as a disciple of Jesus was such an honour. It was wonderful reaching out to the community. We handed out food parcels and Bibles but more importantly we spread the love and knowledge of Jesus. Being around people who have the same love for Jesus is such a blessing and the team was truly an inspiration to both of us. The youth on the destiny team had such a passion for Jesus and watching them interact with the community brought such joy to my heart. We met with Neil and Michelle, our hosts, and they treated us like family. It felt as if we had known them and their precious family for years. They welcomed us into their home which they share along with their 12 adopted children and two biological sons.

We visited three churches during our stay and I was humbled by the experience. I grew within myself and couldn't have asked for kinder people to go on the trip with. Kelsey and I were both requested to pray for people. On the Saturday, I was requested to pray for a 16-year-old girl, Fezeka, who was very sick and at the time was barely able to walk. I joined Pastor Bongani and the leader of the destiny team and we prayed fervently for the young girl and continued to pray against any attack from the enemy on her life. I checked up on her a few times during the afternoon and continued to pray for her healing. When we left, Fezeka was still lying down in the caravan, still unwell and with a high temperature. Even though we did not witness instant results, we all put our trust and faith in Jesus to heal the young girl and we did not lose hope. Neil sent us a message early Monday morning which he had received from Pastor Bongani to advise that Fezeka was better and had gone to school that day – all praise and glory to the Lord! I was taught valuable lessons on the journey, one of them being obedience to that small voice when being prompted to pray for others and remembering that it is all for the glory of Jesus.

During the Sunday service, a Bible passage in Mark 12 popped into my mind where the widow gave her last two copper coins, worth only a few cents, to the treasury and I thought I should put in all my money that I had brought along for the trip into the offering basket, but then I had second thoughts. I gave Kelsey some money to put in the offering basket and I also put money in, but held back on a few rand as I thought about our trip home and that I would need to buy lunch for both of us. Kelsey asked me a few minutes later if I had money left for lunch as clearly it was a concern for her as well, to which I replied, "Yes, I do".

After our sad goodbyes, we drove off onto the gravel road with the stunning backdrop of Swaziland to our left and I had such peace. Gladness filled my heart. What amazing people we had met and I knew I would never be the same.

As we approached the pit stop, I saw the puzzle piece on the concrete wall which we had taken a photograph of on our way to Ingwavuma and I asked Kelsey to send the picture to me. A message then came over the two-way radio system that lunch was taken care of. Only the next morning did I realise that I should have been obedient to the Holy Spirit's prompting about putting in all the money I had that day into the offering as God had already taken care of my worry about the lunch. We need to trust in all His ways and promises. As I stared out the window, the rain was falling and flying ants came out of the soil. As I watched, I noticed the mouse birds in a formation on the fence and, as the insects emerged, they were ready and waiting to pop them into their beaks. God provides. I sat back and just smiled at how God was teaching me His ways.

Early Monday morning, I posted the picture of the puzzle piece on my WhatsApp status update. One of my favourite pastimes is building puzzles. I love puzzles and, under the picture, I wrote that Jesus was my missing puzzle piece and that He has now made me complete. During my prayer time a little later, I felt the Holy Spirit reveal to me that we actually are all puzzle pieces. I am a tiny piece of His puzzle – a gigantic puzzle – and no eye can even imagine how big it is. He is busy constructing His Church and we all fit together. Each puzzle piece is called to build and construct the puzzle by collecting and looking for the missing pieces. No-one likes to build a puzzle only to find one piece missing at the end. It's heartbreaking and I usually throw the puzzle away as it's not complete. That's why Jesus wants no missing pieces in His puzzle. Only once the entire puzzle is completed and all the pieces are in place shall we meet our Maker. By working together as a team and encouraging one another along the way, we can construct and build the puzzle faster. All I can say is, *"Thank You, Jesus, that You chose this puzzle piece to be part of Your perfect picture."*

Conclusion

I have so many stories of miracles to relay but I will leave it for another day. I truly recommend that you start your own prayer book to build your faith and watch how God truly moves in your life. Be filled with His Word, our Sword, and listen to what He teaches us. I find it so incredible that I feel like I have a direct line to God because of the Cross; because of what He did for us.

What's more incredible is that each and every one of us has the opportunity to have that personal relationship with Him – our Father in Heaven – that is what He longs for.

At the heart of the gospel message is a transforming experience. Clint and I both most assuredly needed transformation. The Holy Spirit transformed both Clint and me in our hearts as well as our minds. Many have said that our change was a choice but we know that it was the work of God's grace and the working of the Holy Spirit. God knows exactly what is in our hearts. We can fool creation but we cannot fool the Creator.

We actually don't choose God. God chooses us. He has a personal interest in us and He prompts us to seek Him and whispers in our hearts. He draws us closer to Him as a caring parent but will most assuredly discipline us when needed, as I fully experienced.

I also realised the important role that tears would play in my salvation and in making me whole again. I think that the touch of God in our lives is marked by tears. When we finally let the Holy Spirit into our innermost places, where our darkest secrets are kept, our reaction is to cry, to break down our barriers and to surrender ourselves to our Creator, the Great I AM.

We became devoted Christians and followers of our Lord and Saviour, Jesus Christ. By the supernatural encounter that we both experienced, we had a new birth and, by this, we say joyfully today that we were born again.

The Bible also tells us in Philippians 1:6 that *"He who has begun a good work in you will complete it until the day of Jesus Christ"*. May the Lord continue to use us for His glory.

If you haven't already committed your life to Jesus Christ, why not start your own story today? He is the Author and Finisher of our faith who has endured the Cross, is seated at the right hand of God and is returning one day as He promises.

In closing, I'd like to elaborate on this simple yet powerful, defining and controversial scripture from God's Word in John 14:6 where Jesus makes a claim of exclusivity in order to reach God, the Father.

Other religions and beliefs teach that there are other ways to get to God and to Heaven. However, according to the words of Jesus, He clearly says that He is the **ONLY WAY** and He further says that **NO-ONE** goes to the Father **EXCEPT THROUGH HIM.**

Thus, one can either reject this or accept it. We have the choice to either believe Jesus, that He is telling us the truth, or we can reject this and make Him out to be a liar, believing that it's not the truth.

I choose to believe God's Word.

We have a new heart and a new story filled with joy and peace. We found the way – JESUS IS THE WAY.

Amazing Grace – *"I once was lost but now I'm found, was blind but now I see".*

Looking back at the day I gave my life to Christ on 12th November 2018 – Clint told me this:

> 'You've got a new story to write and it looks nothing like your past'.

I am loving my new story and I trust that Jesus gets all the glory.

Holiday Snaps!

Afriski, Lesotho – July 2013

New York, USA – December 2017

Disneyworld, Florida USA – July 2010

Bahamas – December 2017

Hollywood, LA – September 2015

Los Angeles, USA – September 2015

London – September 2008

Singapore – January 2014

Venice, Italy – June 2012

Tennis Tournament in Dubai – February 2013

FINDING the WAY
Mary-Ann Mey

www.ingramcontent.com/pod-product-compliance
Lightning Source LLC
Chambersburg PA
CBHW071658090426
42738CB00009B/1578